SERIES

A life-changing encounter
with God's Word from the book of

EZEKIEL

D0166750

NAVPRESS

A NavPress resource published in alliance
with Tyndale House Publishers, Inc.

NAVPRESS⬤

NavPress is the publishing ministry of The Navigators, an international Christian organization and leader in personal spiritual development. NavPress is committed to helping people grow spiritually and enjoy lives of meaning and hope through personal and group resources that are biblically rooted, culturally relevant, and highly practical.

For more information, visit www.NavPress.com.

CONTENTS

HOW TO USE THIS GUIDE

Along with all the volumes in the LIFECHANGE series of Bible studies, this guide to Ezekiel shares common goals:

1. To provide you with a firm foundation of understanding, plus a thirst to return to Ezekiel throughout your life.

2. To give you study patterns and skills that help you explore every part of the Bible.

3. To offer you historical background, word definitions, and explanation notes to aid your study.

4. To help you grasp as a whole the message of Ezekiel.

5. To teach you how to let God's Word transform you into Christ's image.

As you begin

This guide includes twelve lessons that will take you chapter by chapter through all of Ezekiel. Each lesson is designed to take from one to two hours of preparation to complete on your own. To benefit most from this time, here's a good way to begin your work on each lesson:

1. Pray for God's help to keep you mentally alert and spiritually sensitive.

2. Read attentively the entire passage mentioned in the lesson's title. (You may want to read the passage from two or more Bible versions—perhaps at least once from a more literal translation such as the New International Version, English Standard Version, New American Standard Bible, or New King James Version and perhaps once more in a paraphrase such as *The Message* or the New Living Translation.) Do your reading in an environment that's as free as possible from distractions. Allow your mind and heart to meditate on the words you encounter—words that are God's personal gift to you and to all His people.

After reading the passage, you're ready to dive into the numbered questions in this guide that make up the main portion of each lesson. Each of these questions is followed by blank space for writing your answers. (This act of writing your answers helps clarify your thinking and stimulates your mental engagement with the passage as well as your later recall.) Use extra paper or a notebook if the space for recording your answers seems too cramped. Continue through the questions in numbered order. If any question seems too difficult or unclear, just skip it and go on to the next.

Each of these questions will typically direct you back to Ezekiel to look again at a certain portion of the assigned passage for that lesson. (At this point, be sure to use a more literal Bible translation rather than a paraphrase.)

As you look closer at a passage, it's helpful to approach it in this progression:

Observe. What does the passage actually *say?* Ask God to help you see it clearly. Notice everything that's there.

Interpret. What does the passage *mean?* Ask God to help you understand. And remember that any passage's meaning is fundamentally determined by its *context.* So stay alert to all you'll see about the setting and background of Ezekiel, and keep thinking of this book as a whole while you proceed through it chapter by chapter. You'll be progressively building up your insights and familiarity with what it's all about.

Apply. Keep asking yourself, *How does this truth affect my life?* (Pray for God's help as you examine yourself in light of that truth and in light of His purpose for each passage.)

Try to consciously follow all three of these steps as you shape your written answer to each question in the lesson.

The extras

In addition to the regular numbered questions you see in this guide, each lesson also offers several "optional" questions or suggestions that appear in the margins. All of these will appear under one of three headings:

Optional Application. These are suggested options for application. Consider these with prayerful sensitivity to the Lord's guidance.

For Thought and Discussion. Many of these questions address various ethical issues and other biblical principles that lead to a wide range of implications. They tend to be particularly suited for group discussion.

For Further Study. These often include cross-references to other parts of the Bible that shed light on a topic in the lesson, plus questions that delve deeper into the passage.

(For additional help for more effective Bible study, refer to the "Study Aids" section starting on page 187.)

6

Changing your life

Don't let your study become an exercise in knowledge alone. Treat the passage as *God's* Word and stay in dialogue with Him as you study. Pray, "Lord, what do You want me to notice here?" "Father, why is this true?" "Lord, how does my life measure up to this?"

Let biblical truth sink into your inner convictions so you'll be increasingly able to act on this truth as a natural way of living.

At times, you may want to consider memorizing a certain verse or passage you come across in your study, one that particularly challenges or encourages you. To help with that, write down the words on a card to keep with you and set aside a few minutes each day to think about the passage. Recite it to yourself repeatedly, always thinking about its meaning. Return to it as often as you can, for a brief review. You'll soon find the words coming to mind spontaneously, and they'll begin to affect your motives and actions.

For group study

Exploring Scripture together in a group is especially valuable for the encouragement, support, and accountability it provides as you seek to apply God's Word to your lives. Together you can listen jointly for God's guidance, pray for each other, help one another resist temptation, and share the spiritual principles you're learning to put into practice. Together you affirm that growing in faith, hope, and love is important and that you need each other in the process.

A group of four to ten people allows for the closest understanding of each other and the richest discussions in Bible study, but you can adapt this guide for groups of other sizes. It will suit a wide range of group types, such as home Bible studies, growth groups, and church classes. Both new and mature Christians will benefit from the guide, regardless of their previous experience in Bible study.

Aim for a positive atmosphere of acceptance, honesty, and openness. In your first meeting, explore candidly everyone's expectations and goals for your time together.

A typical schedule for group study is to take one lesson per week, but feel free to split lessons if you want to discuss them more thoroughly. Or omit some questions in a lesson if your preparation or discussion time is limited. (Group members can always study further on their own at a later time.)

When you come together, you probably won't have time to discuss all the questions in the lesson, so it's helpful for the leader to choose ahead of time the ones to be covered thoroughly. This is one of the main responsibilities a group leader typically assumes.

Each lesson in this guide ends with a section called "For the group." It gives advice for that particular lesson on how to focus the discussion, how to apply the lesson to daily life, and so on. Reading each lesson's "For the group" section ahead of time can help the leader be more effective in guiding the group.

You'll get the greatest benefit from your time together if each group member also prepares ahead of time by writing out his or her answers to each question in the lesson. The private reflection and prayer this preparation can stimulate will be especially important in helping everyone discern how God wants to apply each lesson to your daily lives.

There are many ways to structure the group meeting, and you may want to vary your routine occasionally to help keep things fresh.

Here are some of the elements you can consider including as you come together for each lesson:

Pray together. It's good to pause for prayer as you begin your time together as well as to incorporate a later more extensive time of prayer for each other, after you've had time to share personal needs and prayer requests (you may want to write these down in a notebook). When you begin with prayer, it's worthwhile and honoring to God to ask especially for His Holy Spirit's guidance of your time together.

Worship. Some groups like to sing together and worship God with prayers of praise.

Review. You may want to take time to discuss what difference the previous week's lesson has made in your lives as well as recall the major emphasis you discovered in the passage for that week.

Read the passage aloud. Once you're ready to focus attention together on the assigned Scripture passage in the week's lesson, read it aloud. (One person could do this, or the reading could be shared.)

Open up for questions. Allow time for group members to mention anything in the passage they may have particular questions about.

Summarize the passage. Have one or two people offer a summary of what the passage says.

Discuss. This will be the heart of your time together and will likely take the biggest portion of your time. Focus on the questions you see as the most important and most helpful. Allow and encourage everyone to be part of the discussion for each question. You may want to take written notes as the discussion proceeds. Ask follow-up questions to sharpen your attention and deepen your understanding of what you discuss. You may want to give special attention to the questions in the margins under the heading "For Thought and Discussion." Remember that sometimes these can be especially good for discussion, but be prepared for widely differing answers and opinions. As you hear each other, keep in mind each other's various backgrounds, personalities, and ways of thinking. You can practice godly discernment without ungodly judgment in your discussion.

Encourage further personal study. You can find more opportunities for exploring this lesson's themes and issues under the heading "For Further Study" in the margins throughout the lesson. You can also pursue some of these together during your group time.

Focus on application. Look especially at the "Optional Application" listed in the margins throughout the lesson. Keep encouraging one another in the continual work of adjusting your lives to the truths God gives in Scripture.

8

Summarize your discoveries. You may want to read aloud through the passage one last time together, using the opportunity to solidify your understanding and appreciation of it and clarify how the Lord is speaking to you through it.

Look ahead. Glance together at the headings and questions in the next lesson to see what's coming next.

Give thanks to God. It's good to end your time together by pausing to express gratitude to God for His Word and the work of His Spirit in your minds and hearts during your time together.

Get to know each other better. In early sessions together, you may want to spend time establishing trust, common ground, and a sense of each other's background and what each person hopes to gain from the study. This may help you later with honest discussion about how the Bible applies to each of you. Understanding each other better will make it easier to share about personal applications.

Keep these worthy guidelines in mind throughout your time together:

Let us consider how we may spur one another on toward love and good deeds.

(HEBREWS 10:24)

Carry each other's burdens, and in this way you will fulfill the law of Christ.

(GALATIANS 6:2)

Accept one another, then, just as Christ accepted you, in order to bring praise to God.

(ROMANS 15:7)

THE BOOK OF EZEKIEL

God Responds to His People's Greatest Need

The book of Ezekiel is a book of extremes — scathing and stop-at-nothing in its portrayal of sin, yet vastly, soaringly gracious and positive in its offer of hope to all God's people. In it, God speaks to people whose lives were torn apart by their own and others' sins. Ezekiel pulls no punches in detailing what they were doing wrong, but he also portrays a God who is much, much bigger than His people's sins. This God promises to restore the nation not because the people will repent, but solely because He will offer them grace. He invites them to respond to that grace with repentance.

Background

Ezekiel lived "during a time of international upheaval."[1] When Ezekiel was born, the Assyrian Empire controlled much of the Middle East. Then Assyria crumbled under the pressure of a rising power, Babylon. King Nebuchadnezzar of Babylon was a seemingly unstoppable general. His territory soon included Ezekiel's country: Judah, part of the Promised Land and home to the Judeans or Jews.

In 597 BC, the king of Judah rebelled against Babylon. Nebuchadnezzar squashed the revolt and took ten thousand Jews as exiles to Babylon. Among these exiles was Ezekiel, then in his twenties.

When the book of Ezekiel opens four years later (593 BC), Ezekiel is with the Jewish captives in Babylon. Most of their countrymen are still in Judah, now a vassal state under Babylon's control. The Jews both in exile and back home in Jerusalem hope that the Exile will soon end, that the captives will be able to go home, and that Jerusalem will be spared from any further warfare. False prophets both in exile and back home are encouraging these hopes. Ezekiel reveals that they are tragically mistaken but also points to a greater hope.

The timeline below highlights some of the major dates preceding and during the time of Ezekiel (some dates are approximate).

11

Assyria conquers Israel (the northern kingdom) and exiles the Israelite population.	722 BC
Assyria attacks Judah (the southern kingdom) and Jerusalem but is defeated through God's supernatural intervention (see Isaiah 36–37).	701
Estimated year of the birth of Ezekiel in Judea.	623
The Babylonians begin to conquer Assyrian territory.	616
Nineveh, Assyria's greatest city, falls to the Babylonians.	612
Judah's King Josiah is killed in the battle of Megiddo by Egyptian forces. The Egyptians dominate Judah, placing Jehoiakim on the throne.	609
Battle of Carchemish—Babylon defeats an alliance of Assyrians and Egyptians. Judah gives allegiance to the new power, Babylon. Some Judean nobles (including Daniel and his three friends) are taken captive to Babylon. Nebuchadnezzar becomes king in Babylon.	605
Jehoiakim rebels against the Babylonians, but his revolt is crushed and he is killed. Jehoiachin becomes Judah's king, but he, too, resists Babylon and seeks help from Egypt.	598
Nebuchadnezzar sends an armed force to deal with Jerusalem. Jehoiachin and about 10,000 Jews (including Ezekiel) are exiled to Babylon. Nebuchadnezzar places Zedekiah on Judah's throne. Zedekiah submits to Babylon for about a decade. Then he, too, rebels.	597
Ezekiel's first vision and call from God (see Ezekiel 1–3).	593
Ezekiel transported by the Spirit to Jerusalem to view abominations in the temple (see Ezekiel 8:1).	592
God gives Ezekiel an oracle outlining Israel's evil history (see Ezekiel 20:1).	591
Zedekiah rebels, and the Babylonians lay siege to Jerusalem (see Ezekiel 24:1).	588
Ezekiel's oracles against Tyre and Egypt (see Ezekiel 26:1; 29:1; 30:20; 31:1).	587–586
Jerusalem falls to the Babylonians, and the city and temple are burned (see Ezekiel 33:21). Zedekiah is slain.	586

Ezekiel's lament over Pharaoh (see Ezekiel 32:1,17).	585
Ezekiel's vision of the future temple and holy city (see Ezekiel 40:1).	573
Ezekiel given a later oracle concerning Nebuchadnezzar, Egypt, and Tyre (see Ezekiel 29:17).	571

Structure and arrangement

We can outline the book of Ezekiel like this:

(I) Chapters 1–24. Ezekiel is called to be a prophet. He offers words and signs of judgment from God against His people.
(II) Chapters 25–32. God speaks of judgment against Israel's neighbors.
(III) Chapters 33–48. Ezekiel learns of the final fall of Jerusalem, the fulfillment of the judgment he predicted. He now sees past that judgment and offers teaching and encouragement for God's people regarding their future. The final chapters of this encouragement (chapters 40–48) are an extended vision from God of a new temple, a new city, and a new land of Israel.

Like other Old Testament prophetic books, such as Isaiah, the book moves generally from judgment against the prophet's own nation, to judgment against other nations, to future blessings for those who believe in God. Within each section of the book, the visions and oracles are not collected in a linear or chronological order. Each section is more like an album of separate photos than like a continuous video.

Ezekiel the man

When the book opens, Ezekiel is thirty years old, married, a homeowner, and brought up to be a priest. He is just starting his priestly ministry, although because he is more than a thousand miles from the temple in Jerusalem, he can't do the main job of a priest: offer sacrifices. At this turning point in his life, God calls him to be a prophet.

He is roughly the same age as Daniel. Years ago, back in Jerusalem, he probably heard the prophet Jeremiah. Jeremiah is still speaking to the Jews in Judah when Ezekiel takes up the same calling to the Jews in exile.

Being God's prophet proves to be a grueling job. God asks Ezekiel not just to speak for Him, but to act out God's terrible messages in ways that are, sometimes degrading and sometimes heartbreaking. The Jews don't want to hear what Ezekiel has to say, and he bears in silence the knowledge that his beloved Jerusalem is going to be turned to rubble. God even asks him not to openly grieve the death of his wife so that he can share God's sorrow in the death of the nation that was God's bride.

Ezekiel is consistently obedient to God through all of this, while also transparently revealing his reactions, emotions, and questions. His dependent trust in the Lord gives him strength, fearlessness, and faithfulness.

1. *NIV Study Bible* (Grand Rapids, MI: Zondervan, 1985), introduction to Ezekiel: "Background."

EZEKIEL 1-3

Encountering God and His Call

1. One of the best guidelines for getting the most from Ezekiel is found in 2 Timothy 3:16-17, words which Paul wrote with the Old Testament first in view. He said that *all* Scripture is of great benefit to (a) teach us, (b) rebuke us, (c) correct us, and (d) train us in righteousness. Paul added that these Scriptures completely equip the person of God "for every good work." As you think seriously about those guidelines, in which of these areas do you especially want to experience the usefulness of Ezekiel? Express your desire in a written prayer to God.

   To be obedient to Share what God directs me to do - share the gospel - even to the rebellious.

   Father, Please use me - in spite of my stubbornness, to share your love w/ the unloving & rebellious people you put in my path.

2. In Jeremiah 23:29, God says that His Word is "like fire" and "like a hammer." He can use the Scriptures to burn away unclean thoughts and desires in our hearts. He can also use Scripture, with hammer-like hardness, to crush and crumble our spiritual hardness. From your study of Ezekiel, how do you most want to see the fire-and-hammer power of God's Word at work in your own life? Again, express this longing in a written prayer to God.

_to be
diligent &
retain the
info. for
future
reference._

_To be more like Jesus –
no matter the cost.
Open my heart & eyes
to your ways Jesus._

3. Think about these words of Paul to his younger
   helper Timothy: "Do your best to present yourself to God as one approved, a worker who does
   not need to be ashamed and who correctly han-
   dles the word of truth" (2 Timothy 2:15). As you
   study God's word of truth in Ezekiel, He calls
   you to be a "worker." It takes *work*—concentra-
   tion and perseverance—to fully appropriate
   God's blessings for us in this book. Express here
   your commitment before God to work diligently
   in this study of Ezekiel.

_Father,
Give me the strength
to honor my commitment
in this study._

4. Glance ahead through the pages of Ezekiel. If
   your Bible has headings added into the text,
   scan these headings as you turn the pages.
   What overall impressions of this book do you
   gain?

5. Now go through the first three chapters of
   Ezekiel in one continuous read. Again, what
   overall impressions do you gain?

_God preparing to
destroy thru His
anger & wrath.
Warnings given._

16

Begin your concentrated study with a careful verse-by-verse reading of Ezekiel, and use the following questions and notes to help you process your discoveries.

Ezekiel 1

In my thirtieth year (1:1). Young men descended from Aaron, the brother of Moses, were destined to be priests. Priests offered sacrifices at God's temple in Jerusalem, and they served in other leadership and teaching functions in the community as well. Young men were trained for this role, and then they took up their priestly duties at age thirty (see Numbers 4:3,23,30,39,43; 1 Chronicles 23:3). So Ezekiel received his first vision, commissioning him to be a prophet, in the year when he would have taken up his priestly duties if he had not been exiled from Jerusalem. He was unable to offer sacrifices in Jerusalem, but now he had another task from God. The timing of his calling underlines the book's "priestly atmosphere."[1]

Visions of God (1:1). See also 8:3 and 40:2.

For Further Study:
Explore other Scriptures where God appears in glorious visions. Ezekiel would have been familiar with them. See Exodus 19; 24:15-18; 29:42-46; 40:34-38; Numbers 9:15-23; 14:10; 16:19; 20:6; 1 Kings 8:10-11; 2 Chronicles 5:14; Isaiah 6:3. What links do you see between those passages and Ezekiel's experience related in Ezekiel 1?

Understanding Visions in Scripture

Here are four principles for interpreting visions in the Bible:
   1. Think of the images as you would think of figurative language. Don't take them literally. For example, when the psalmist says, "The Lord is my shepherd," he doesn't mean that he himself is literally a sheep. He means that God relates to him in some ways that are like the way a shepherd relates to a sheep. The "shepherd" image creates a powerful mental picture. In the same way, the living creatures with four faces and four wings in Ezekiel 1 create a powerful mental picture that shows us something about God, angels, and spiritual reality. God doesn't have a literal throne built of creatures and wheels. He

(continued on page 18)

17

(continued from page 17)

appeared to Ezekiel like that in order to teach us something.

2. Try to understand the main idea and emotion the vision conveys. Don't get bogged down interpreting every detail.

3. Pay attention to the interpretation the text itself gives about the vision. The Bible text will often explain what the vision means. The explanation usually emphasizes the big picture, not the details.

4. Look for parallel Bible passages. The prophets often try to apply past Scriptures to their present reality. The prophets also have basically one shared message about judgment and redemption that they convey in their various voices.[2]

On the fifth of the month—it was the fifth year of the exile of King Jehoiachin (1:2). July 593 BC.[3] More than ten times, Ezekiel tells us the precise date on which he received a vision. No other prophet does this. He was aware of how his visions were relevant to precise events back in Jerusalem. The visions came between 593 and 573 BC. They cover the last seven years of Jerusalem's survival as a place of life and worship, and then the first thirteen years of the Jews' grief over Jerusalem's destruction.

6. a. In the opening chapter of Ezekiel, verse 1 and verses 2-3 to some degree appear to be two parallel statements reinforcing each other. What do we learn about Ezekiel here in 1:1-3?

_____

_____

_____

   b. In what way did Ezekiel encounter or experience God?

_____

18

c. How would you relate Ezekiel's phrase "I saw visions of God" in verse 1 with the phrase "the word of the LORD came to Ezekiel" in verse 3?

Saw - heard - & felt

For Thought and Discussion: If some Christians today were somehow allowed to see exactly what Ezekiel saw in chapter 1, what impact do you think it would likely have on them?

For Further Study: Compare Ezekiel 1:4-5 with Psalm 18:9-14; 97:2; Nahum 1:3. What do you think the image of God riding on a storm is meant to convey about Him?

___

The hand of the LORD was on him (1:3). A similar phrase is used repeatedly in passages describing Ezekiel's visions. See also 3:14,22; 8:1; 37:1; and 40:1.

7. Describe what Ezekiel sees first in 1:4.

a great cloud with lightning & fire

___

Four living creatures (1:5). These are later called "cherubim" (see Ezekiel 10:1-5,15,20). Cherubim guard God's holiness and enforce His judgment. For instance, when Adam and Eve were exiled from the Garden of Eden, cherubim were sent to guard the way back to the Tree of Life (see Genesis 3:24).[4] Ezekiel would have seen cherubim depicted in the Jerusalem temple (see Exodus 25–26; 36–37; 1 Kings 6; 2 Chronicles 3).

___

8. What seem to be the most important features of the four living creatures that Ezekiel sees in 1:5-14?

_____

Wherever the spirit would go, they would go
(1:12). In this context, a vision of God's glorious presence, the "spirit" is probably the Holy Spirit, God Himself.

_____

9. What seem to be the most important features of the wheels that Ezekiel sees in 1:15-21?

_____

_____

_____

10. a. In 1:22-25, what else does Ezekiel *see* in regard to the four living creatures?

_____

_____

_____

b. What does Ezekiel *hear* in these verses?

_____

_____

11. What is most significant in what Ezekiel sees and hears in 1:26-28?

_____

_____

_____

_____

Like the appearance of a rainbow in the clouds on a rainy day (1:28). The rainbow was a symbol of hope, of God's mercy and faithfulness despite a storm of judgment (see Genesis 9:12-16). In the midst of this terrifying vision, there

20

is a glimmer of hope. God has a covenant with His people, and that covenant says He must judge sin. But He will not destroy His people completely.

This was the appearance of the likeness of the glory of the LORD (1:28). The "glory" of the Lord was His radiant presence. In the days of Moses He manifested His glory in a pillar of cloud by day and a pillar of fire by night. This vision isn't a face-to-face experience of the glory, but the appearance of its likeness — an echo of it — and even that is enough to flatten Ezekiel. The revelation of God's glory is a theme running through this book.

I fell facedown (1:28). Terror and falling down are a common response to beholding the holy God (see Isaiah 6:1-5; Revelation 1:10-18). It's right to be terrified of God's judgment. Falling facedown also indicates humility — Ezekiel doesn't obstinately resist the revelation, but takes a lowly posture.

A Movement-Filled Vision

Isaiah saw the Lord seated on a throne in the temple (see Isaiah 6:1-7). Ezekiel sees the Lord on a throne, but the throne is not in the temple. Here the Lord is not fixed in the place where the priests are used to serving Him, but out on the move in the land where He is sending His people into exile. As in the book of Job, He moves in a "windstorm" (Ezekiel 1:4; compare Job 38:1). He's not asleep or tame or trapped in the building the priests control. He's alive and dangerous. He is visiting His exiled people not to rescue them and make everything all right, but to give a warning that even more judgment is yet to come, because the people haven't repented. In Ezekiel 10, the prophet will see another vision of God's glory abandoning His temple altogether so that the Babylonians can smash it.

For Further Study: In summarizing this vision recorded in Ezekiel 1, the prophet says, "This was the appearance of the likeness of the glory of the LORD" (1:28). Compare this with how others in Scripture encountered God's glory in these passages: Exodus 16:6-12; 19:16-25; 24:15-18; 33:18-23; 34:5-8; Numbers 16:16-35; 1 Kings 8:10-11; Isaiah 6:1-7; Daniel 10:1-19; Revelation 4:1-11.

Optional Application: With Ezekiel 1 in mind, what do you think God most wants you to understand about His glory — and to praise Him for? Offer Him that praise now.

21

Optional Application: Review the specifics of Ezekiel's call in chapters 2 and 3. How might these specifics relate to what God has called you to do?

12. Look back over Ezekiel's vision in 1:4-28. In what specific ways does Ezekiel see motion here?

_____

_____

_____

Ezekiel 2 and 3

13. Ezekiel's call is presented to us in chapters 2 and 3. What specific things does God tell Ezekiel to do or to *not do*?

_____

_____

_____

_____

Son of man (2:1). God calls Ezekiel "son of man" more than ninety times. The title means "human" and emphasizes Ezekiel's mere humanness — his frailty, mortality, lowliness — compared with God's holy glory and the cherubims' heavenly majesty. The title reminds Ezekiel that he is totally dependent on the Spirit's power, that in his mere humanness alone he couldn't hope to receive God's message and deliver it with authority. When Jesus calls Himself "Son of Man" in the Gospels, the title retains some of this humility — the Son of God has laid aside His divine privileges, humbling Himself to become fully human. But Jesus' use of the term owes more to Daniel 7:13-14, where the "one like a son of man" is given sovereign power and is served as Messiah.

14. a. In this lengthy passage on Ezekiel's call (chapters 2 and 3), in what ways does God demonstrate His grace?

_____

_____

_____

_____

b. In what ways does He demonstrate His holiness in these two chapters?

_____

_____

_____

For Thought and Discussion: God sent Ezekiel to speak to an audience of rebels, and He warned His prophet not to be afraid or discouraged because of their opposition or lack of response. Does the need for such a warning indicate any weakness on Ezekiel's part? Why or why not?

I am sending you to the Israelites, to a rebellious nation (2:3). Instead of calling them "my people," the ones with whom He has a covenant, God calls them literally "sons of Israel," the true heirs of a rebellious man. This is not a happy sign.

They are a rebellious people (2:5). In this passage (2:1–3:15) that presents Ezekiel's call, Israel is called a "rebellious people" six times (in 2:5-8; 3:9; 3:26-27).

For Thought and Discussion: In what ways, if any, might God's description of Israel as a "rebellious people" (2:5-8; 3:9; 3:26-27) be correctly applied to God's people today?

Optional Application: In whatever God has called you to do, how has He let you know of any difficulties or hardships to expect?

For Thought and Discussion: Ezekiel was told to speak God's message even if people closed their ears to his words (see 2:5). How does this relate and apply to those who are called to preach and teach God's Word today?

God often launched the ministries of Old Testament prophets with visions of His glory. These first visions stuck in their minds, and when they hit tough times, they drew strength from the memory. Today, too, we need to base our lives and ministries on a "divine confrontation,"[5] an understanding or experience of God's glory that is more than just intellectual. Only by knowing God's magnificence at our core can we humbly serve Him through the ups and downs of life. We may not have a vision or an emotional experience, but we need the Holy Spirit

Optional Application: In what sense and to what degree have you experienced an encounter with God and His glory that has helped define your understanding of what He wants you to do with your life? What difference has this made?

For Further Study: Partaking of God's Word, Ezekiel found it to be "as sweet as honey" (3:3). How does that relate to what is taught in these passages: Psalm 19:10; 119:103; Proverbs 16:24; 24:13-14; Jeremiah 15:16?

to stamp our hearts with a true awareness of God's reality and His character.

"Son of man, eat this scroll. . . ." So I ate it (3:3). Throughout most of the vision, Ezekiel is just a spectator. In this moment he is told to act, and he acts. The scroll is God's Word, and not a very tasty Word, but he obediently digests it so that he can later speak it to the exiles.

Ezekiel is consistently humble and obedient to God's Word. God appears and he falls on his face. God speaks and he listens. God tells him to stand and he stands. He is able to obey — to stand and hear God — only because the Spirit enables him. He will be able to speak to the exiles because the Spirit will empower him. When the vision is over, he sits for a week (see 3:15), unable to do anything without the Spirit.

"More than any other prophet, Ezekiel is a prophet of the Spirit. . . . Ezekiel not only spoke of the power of the Spirit; he embodied the Spirit's power in his own person."[6]

15. How would you summarize and explain Ezekiel's response to his calling, as we see it recorded in 3:14-15?

_____

_____

_____

_____

The strong hand of the LORD on me (3:14). See also 3:22. Recall the similar wording in 1:3.

Bitterness (3:14). Anguish, distress. It gives Ezekiel no pleasure to convey the Word he's been given.

I came to the exiles. . . . I sat among them (3:15). He doesn't stand above or apart from the exiles. He doesn't speak from some safe, comfortable place. He shares the devastation of all they've lost and all they fear to lose.

For Thought and Discussion: What do you think it means experientially for someone to sense, as Ezekiel did, "the strong hand of the LORD on me" (3:14)?

For Thought and Discussion: We read in 3:15 of Ezekiel's being overwhelmed for a week by what he had just seen and heard. What kinds of thoughts do you imagine were going through his mind?

16. When the Lord made Ezekiel a "watchman" for Israel, what significant responsibilities did this bring, according to 3:16-21?

_____

_____

_____

Watchman (3:17). A sentry who stands on the city wall, watching for dangers from outside or inside, so that he can warn the citizens.

Get up and go out to the plain (3:22). Or, "Arise, go out into the valley" (ESV) — the broad river valley between the Tigris and Euphrates rivers in what is now Iraq. The vision of dry bones (see 37:1) will take place here.[7]

17. In 3:22-27 . . .

a. What does the Lord ask Ezekiel to do?

_____

_____

_____

b. What does the Lord say will happen to Ezekiel?

_____

25

For Thought and Discussion: God made Ezekiel a watchman to give warning to His people. Does God give warnings to His people today? If so, how?

For Further Study: Keeping in mind Ezekiel's God-given role as a watchman, compare this to other prophets who served as watchmen. What else do you learn about the biblical concept of a watchman as seen in these passages: Isaiah 21:6-12; 62:6-7; Jeremiah 6:16-17; 31:5-6? Also, in the New Testament, how is this function served by church leaders, according to the instruction in Acts 20:28-31 and Hebrews 13:17?

c. How might these things deepen Ezekiel's calling as God's prophet and spokesman and his dependence on God?

I fell facedown. Then the Spirit . . . raised me to my feet (3:23-24). See Ezekiel's similar experience seven days earlier in 1:28 and 2:1.

Ezekiel has not been shown the promise of judgment for his own curiosity. He has been sent on a mission of life and death. Those who hear him and repent will live; those who reject him will die. He isn't responsible for results. He is responsible for obedience, for giving the warning, despite the price he may pay.

The Spirit . . . spoke to me and said: "Go, shut yourself inside your house. And you, son of man, they will tie with ropes. . . . I will make your tongue stick to the roof of your mouth" (3:24-26). Ezekiel is going to be a living picture of the exiles' captivity. His imprisonment will be self-inflicted ("Go, shut yourself") and inflicted by others ("they will tie") and caused by God ("I will make"). With all three of these causes at once, there will be no escape, no deciding to end it.[8]

You will be silent. . . . But when I speak to you, I will open your mouth (3:26-27). For seven and a half years, until the destruction of Jerusalem,

Ezekiel would be unable to speak — except on the handful of occasions when God gave him a message to deliver. His muteness would set him apart from the many prophets who spoke constantly, and it would make his rare speeches all the more dramatic in hopes of striking his hearers to the heart.

Optional Application: Ezekiel 3 emphasizes the prophet's dependence on God and His Spirit in order to accomplish what God called him to do. In a personally meaningful way, how would you express the same kind of need and dependence in your own life?

18. What would you select as the key verse or passage in Ezekiel 1–3 — one that best captures or reflects the dynamics of what these chapters are all about?

_____

_____

_____

19. List any lingering questions you have about Ezekiel 1–3.

_____

_____

_____

_____

For the group

(In your first meeting, it may be helpful to turn to the front of this book and review together "How to Use This Guide" starting on page 5.)

You may want to focus your discussion for lesson 1 especially on the following issues, themes, and concepts (which are recognized as major overall themes in Ezekiel). How are they further developed in chapters 1–3?

- God's glory and sovereignty
- The depth of human sinfulness
- The certainty, nature, and purpose of God's judgment against sin
- The nature of God's covenant relationship with His people
- The promise of mercy and hope for the future

27

The following numbered questions in lesson 1 may stimulate your best and most helpful discussion: 4, 5, 11, 14, 16, 18, and 19.

Look also at the questions in the margins under the headings "For Thought and Discussion" and "Optional Application."

1. Ralph H. Alexander, *Ezekiel*, vol. 6 of *The Expositor's Bible Commentary*, ed. Frank E. Gaebelein (Grand Rapids, MI: Zondervan, 1986), 754.
2. Based on Alexander, 756.
3. *ESV Study Bible*, introduction to Ezekiel: "Dates in Ezekiel."
4. Iain M. Duguid, *Ezekiel*, in *The NIV Application Commentary*, ed. Terry Muck (Grand Rapids, MI: Zondervan, 1999), 59.
5. Alexander, 760.
6. Daniel I. Block, *The Book of Ezekiel:* Chapters 1-24, in the *New International Commentary on the Old Testament* (Grand Rapids, MI: Eerdmans, 1997), 50.
7. *ESV Study Bible*, at Ezekiel 3:22-23.
8. Duguid, 80.

EZEKIEL 4–10

God's Case Against Jerusalem and Israel

1. To begin your study in this lesson, read through Ezekiel 4–10 in one sitting. What overall impressions do you gain from the text? What stands out to you most?

_____

_____

_____

_____

_____

_____

Now begin your verse-by-verse study.

The Lord has appeared to Ezekiel in the form of a fiery warrior and commissioned him to take a message of judgment to the exiles and the people of Jerusalem. In chapters 4–5, we find that the Lord's message will not always come in the form of words. Instead, Ezekiel will perform

For Thought and Discussion: In your opinion, what kind of personality traits and character qualities are best for a person called to be God's prophet?

symbolic actions, "sign-acts,"[1] which are explained with words. These sign-acts are humiliating bits of performance art, excruciating to perform and grim to ponder, carrying the Lord's authority. We can only imagine what it was like to have to do these things or see them.

Ezekiel 4

2. Imagine watching Ezekiel do what God tells him to do in each of the following passages. What exactly would you see? Summarize and outline these things.

4:1-3

_____

_____

_____

4:4-8

_____

_____

4:9-12

_____

_____

_____

An iron wall between you and the city (4:3). This represents the spiritual barrier between the Lord and the people. Their sins have made it impossible for them to communicate with Him even if they wanted to.[2]

Lie on your side (4:4). Ezekiel wasn't on his side all day and all night. He fixed meals (see 4:9-15),

30

and 8:1 shows him sitting in his house with the elders during the period when he was lying on his right side. So apparently he spent only part of each day acting out the message.[3]

People of Israel (4:4). The whole covenant people, including all twelve tribes.

390 days (4:5). This symbolizes 390 years of the people's sin. That period began during the reign of King Solomon, when the temple was built, and continued through the long, ugly history recounted in 1 and 2 Kings, when the temple was increasingly profaned by the people's indifference to God.

People of Judah (4:6). God has the exiles from Judah particularly in mind here. Forty years isn't the precise number of the years of their exile, but biblically it's a round number (representing a generation) that reminds one of the forty years of wilderness wandering. Like the exile, the wilderness time was also a punishment for disobedience.

Bear the sin (4:6). Or, "bear the punishment" (ESV). Unlike Christ's bearing of sin, Ezekiel's has no power to cleanse the people of guilt. Ezekiel isn't taking the punishment in their place. Rather, he is identifying with them in order to illustrate their sin.

The total number of days (390+40) of the sign is 430. This corresponds to the 430 years that the Israelites spent in Egypt (see Exodus 12:40). Just as the bondage in Egypt eventually ended in the Exodus and the journey to the Promised Land, so God hints that the exile in Babylon will eventually end. The present generation is under judgment and won't live to see the redemption, but there is hope that their descendants will have a new exodus and return to the land.

31

For Thought and Discussion: God chose to have Ezekiel perform sign-acts (like his actions in chapter 4) to help convey His message. What do you see as the advantages of such a teaching strategy? What might be the disadvantages?

Optional Application: Can you imagine any circumstances in which you would want to protest to the Lord in a way similar to Ezekiel's reaction in 4:14? What can you learn here from Ezekiel's example and from the way God responded to him?

Twenty shekels of food . . . each day (4:10). Half a pound of legumes and grain, plus two-thirds of a quart of water, were barely enough to keep someone alive. These are siege rations.

3. What significance do you see in the interchange between God and Ezekiel in 4:13-15?

_____

_____

_____

Using human excrement for fuel (4:12). The Law of Moses forbade the people — especially the priests — from eating unclean food. God commands Ezekiel to eat unclean food to show how disgusting the siege of Jerusalem will be.

Cow dung instead of human excrement (4:15). God allows Ezekiel to substitute cow dung to maintain his priestly purity. He is like the righteous remnant among the exiles, managing to keep his purity even in an unclean land. Most of the exiles may lose their purity, but by the grace of God and their own faithfulness, some will not.[4]

4. a. Summarize what God promises in 4:16-17.

_____

_____

_____

_____

b. What significance do you see in this promise?

_____

_____

_____

c. What does it reveal about God's character?

_____

_____

_____

For Further Study: Compare Ezekiel's actions in 5:2-4 with the fate of Jerusalem as recorded in these passages: 2 Kings 25:8-21; 2 Chronicles 36:17-21; Jeremiah 52:12-30.

Ezekiel 5

5. Now imagine watching Ezekiel do what God tells him to do in 5:1-4. What exactly would you see?

_____

_____

_____

_____

Shave your head and your beard (5:1). Signifying humiliation and disgrace (see 2 Samuel 10:4-5).

Hair (5:2-3). Representing the people of Jerusalem.

6. a. What specific wrongdoing does God call attention to in 5:5-12?

_____

_____

_____

b. As a result, what does God promise to His people?

_____

_____

_____

This is what the Sovereign LORD says: I myself am against you (5:8). The Lord is now

Optional Application: Review God's words to Jerusalem in Ezekiel 5:8, and compare them with His words to His people in Romans 8:31-32. What gratitude does this comparison bring to your heart and mind? Express that gratitude in prayer.

For Further Study: Study Leviticus 26:14-45. What specific connections with Ezekiel 5:5-17 do you find?

explaining the siege drama of 4:1-2. It is the Lord, not just the Babylonians, who will besiege Jerusalem.

7. What does God promise to do to His people in 5:13-17?

_____

_____

_____

_____

8. What does chapter 5 reveal most about God's character?

_____

_____

_____

_____

With his hair, Ezekiel signifies the disaster coming upon Jerusalem in 5:1-4. In the rest of chapter 5, God explains why. His people have broken their covenant with Him, so the curses of Leviticus 26:14-45 will come to pass. God refers to the covenant to make clear that His judgment is just. The people knew the penalties all along, and He has waited centuries to pass sentence. God hasn't suddenly lost His temper.

The penalties in Leviticus 26 also bring to mind the hope in 26:44-45: "Yet in spite of this, when they are in the land of their enemies, I will not reject them or abhor them so as to destroy them completely, breaking my covenant with them. I am the LORD their God. But for their sake I will remember the covenant with their ancestors whom I brought out of Egypt in the sight of the nations to be their God. I am the LORD." This punishment isn't the end; it will set the stage for God to work yet another amazing redemption.

Ezekiel 6

9. Summarize God's message to His people in each of these sections of chapter 6:

6:1-7

_____

_____

_____

6:8-10

_____

_____

_____

6:11-14

_____

_____

_____

For Thought and Discussion: For a person who fears God and whose heart is still sensitive to the Lord's Spirit, what phrases in God's message in chapter 5 might be the most tragic and grievous?

The mountains of Israel . . . high places (6:2-3). Before there was a temple in Jerusalem, God allowed the people to offer sacrifices on the "high places" or hills. Once the temple was built, it was the only authorized place for sacrifice, and the people were expected to journey there several times a year (see Deuteronomy 12). But they continued to offer sacrifices on their local high places and increasingly mixed in Canaanite gods and practices.

You will know that I am the LORD (6:7). This phrase, or some variation of it, occurs more than fifty times in Ezekiel. It's known as the "recognition formula." The book's main purpose is for Ezekiel's hearers (and us) to know by what happens in history that the Lord really exists and is God. Today we often think we will know God by looking inside ourselves, but here God says we will know Him by truly pondering what He has done.[5]

For Thought and Discussion: Why, from God's perspective, is idolatry so bad?

For Further Study: How is God's attitude in Ezekiel 6:3-5 reflected also in Leviticus 26:30 and Jeremiah 8:1-3?

For Further Study: What happened at Israel's "high places," according to 2 Kings 17:9-11?

Optional Application: Notice the especially personal aspect of the words God speaks in Ezekiel 6:9-10. How do these words relate to what you sense God desires in His relationship with you? Express this in prayer to Him.

10. What significance do you see in the promise from God (the "recognition formula" — see note on 6:7) that's repeated in verses 7, 10, 13, and 14 of chapter 6? What do you think God most wants His people to understand from this statement?

_____

_____

_____

_____

_____

Notice the contrast between 6:8-10 and 6:11-14. There are two possible conclusions to Israel's story: the people can suffer judgment, be motivated to repent, and then be restored; or they can suffer judgment, respond with bitterness, and be utterly wiped out. Either way, God's justice will be shown. They will know that the Lord is God. Each individual who hears Ezekiel also faces these two options: they can respond to suffering by remembering God or by rejecting Him. With remembering Him there is hope; with rejecting Him there is none.[6]

In sending discipline, God's loving desire is always to restore people to Himself, to remind them that He exists. He takes no joy in their suffering.

11. What does chapter 6 reveal about God's character?

_____

_____

_____

_____

_____

Ezekiel 7

12. The repeated formula "You will know that I am the LORD" that we observed in chapter 6 is found again in chapter 7, in verses 4, 9, and 27. What further meaning and significance are given to this phrase in these passages?

_____

_____

_____

_____

For Thought and Discussion: From what you see in chapter 7, what are some of the things God wants us to understand most about His wrath?

The end! (7:2). These two words are repeated five times in 7:1-6 to emphasize that God's patience is truly over and the judgment will be total.

---

13. In God's message to His people in chapter 7, describe the major points made in each of these sections:

7:1-9

_____

_____

_____

7:10-13

_____

_____

_____

7:14-22

_____

_____

_____

For Further Study:
Compare what you
see in Ezekiel 7 with
prophecies concern-
ing the "day of the
LORD" in these pas-
sages: Isaiah 13:6-13;
Jeremiah 46:10;
Joel 1:15; 2:1,11,31;
3:14; Amos 5:18-20;
8:9-10; Obadiah 15;
Zephaniah 1:7,14;
Malachi 4:5.

7:23-27

_____

_____

_____

*The end is now upon you. . . . The time has
    come* (7:3,7). What was coming has now come.
    This chapter has no glimpse of the hope that
    was apparent in previous chapters.

*I will not look on you with pity; I will not spare
    you. . . . Then you will know that I am the
    LORD* (7:4). Again God emphasizes that even
    when He is showing no mercy, His loving pur-
    pose is still for His people to know Him.

See, the day! (7:10). "The day of the LORD" was
    a common expectation of the people. They
    expected it to be a day when God judged the
    nations who were against them. Many of the
    prophets allude to this expectation and warn
    that the day of judgment will also fall on God's
    own people.

Let not the buyer rejoice nor the seller grieve
    (7:12). When judgment comes, making money
    will be meaningless; neither good deals nor bad
    deals will matter anymore.

Every leg will be wet with urine (7:17). God isn't
    embarrassed to put things in the most graphic
    terms to get His people's attention.

*Vision from the prophet . . . priestly instruction
    . . . counsel of the elders* (7:26). The leaders
    have all failed to lead properly with their own
    conduct, and now they have nothing useful to
    say at all.

_____

14. What does chapter 7 reveal about God's
    character?

_____

_____

_____

_____

For Thought and Discussion: What does Ezekiel 8 reveal or imply about what God sees us do "in secret"?

Ezekiel 8

Ezekiel 8–11 is all one vision. Ezekiel is taken up by the hair of his head to see Jerusalem in 8:1-3 and is finally deposited back in Babylon in 11:24-25.

In the sixth year, in the sixth month on the fifth day (8:1). September 592 BC,[7] fourteen months after Ezekiel's first vision. He has spent that time performing the sign in chapter 4. Almost 430 days (390 plus 40) have passed, so he is close to finishing that sign.

Elders of Judah (8:1). The leaders of the Jewish exiles in Babylon.

The hand of the Sovereign LORD came on me (8:1). Recall the similar wording in 1:3 and 3:14.

15. Describe the setting for the new vision that Ezekiel experiences in 8:1-2.

_____

_____

_____

16. a. What happens to Ezekiel in 8:3-6, and what do you see as the significance of this?

_____

_____

_____

b. Look also at 8:7-13. What happens — and what is the significance?

_____

_____

_____

c. How does God want Ezekiel to view what he is seeing here?

_____

_____

_____

Idol of jealousy (8:5). Or, "image of jealousy" (ESV). Ezekiel deliberately omits details about exactly what this idol or image was. Possibly his hearers know, or possibly he means to focus on God's response: jealousy — anger that His people are being unfaithful to Him.

Things that will drive me far from my sanctuary (8:6). The Lord isn't leaving because He doesn't care; He's leaving because the people are driving Him away.

What the elders of Israel are doing in the darkness, each at the shrine of his own idol (8:12). These elders who bowed to their secret idols in the darkness had often bowed publicly to God in the temple. "Their true worship was their worship in the dark. The other was conscious or unconscious hypocrisy." A person's true worship is not that which he performs in public, in church. His true worship is what he offers when no one else is looking. "Who is the God to whom in your inmost heart you bow down? What do you do in the dark? That is the question. Whom do you worship there? Your other worship is not worship at all."[8]

---

17. a. What does Ezekiel experience in 8:14-15?

_____

_____

_____

b. How does God want him to view this?

_____

_____

_____

c. What does Ezekiel see in 8:16-18?

_____

_____

_____

d. How does God interpret this for him?

_____

_____

_____

Optional Application: What idols are you tempted to worship? Ask yourself, what do I want most? What do I think would make me happy? What do I fear most? Where does my mind go naturally when it's free to wander?[9]

For Thought and Discussion: At God's command, Ezekiel "dug into the wall" (8:8) at the temple. What do you think might have been going through his mind while he was digging?

Tammuz (8:14). A Babylonian fertility god. Mourning for him was a ritual that celebrated his death, descent to the underworld, and return as a symbol of the annual cycle of nature from winter to summer. Mourning him was supposed to speed the return of fertility.[10]

Bowing down to the sun in the east (8:16). The Law of Moses forbade sun worship because it was worshiping the creation rather than the Creator (see Deuteronomy 4:19). Yet it was a persistent temptation in Judah (see 2 Kings 23:5,11; 2 Chronicles 29:6-7).

---

18. What significance do you see in the phrase that is repeated at the end of verses 6, 13, and 15 in chapter 8?

_____

_____

41

For Thought and Discussion: In God's sight, what practices or attitudes among God's people might correspond to all the "detestable things" ("abominations," ESV) that God shows Ezekiel in chapter 8?

Optional Application: In God's sight, what practices in your own life might correspond to all the "detestable things" or "abominations" that God shows Ezekiel in chapter 8?

Putting the branch to their nose! (8:17). A gesture of defiance.

19. What does God promise to do in 8:17-18 and for what specific reason?

20. What does chapter 8 reveal most about God and His character?

Ezekiel 9

Chapter 8 depicted God's people doing idolatrous practices learned from various nations and involving a buffet of gods: human-shaped gods, animal gods, the sun. In chapter 9 God now judges His people for engaging in multi-faith worship.

21. a. Summarize and outline what Ezekiel hears and sees in 9:1-7.

b. What is Ezekiel's reaction in 9:8?

_____

_____

_____

c. In 9:9-10, as God responds to Ezekiel's reaction, what does He promise and for what reason?

_____

_____

_____

Those who are appointed to execute judgment on the city . . . six men (9:1-2). These may represent angels and/or the human Babylonian invaders.

The land is full of bloodshed and the city is full of injustice (9:9). Recall God's similar charge in 7:23.

They say, "The LORD has forsaken the land; the LORD does not see" (9:9). Their hearts are hardened with this false belief. The judgment will prove that the Lord has seen everything and does in fact care.

---

22. What is the significance of what Ezekiel witnesses in 9:11?

_____

_____

_____

23. What does chapter 9 reveal most about God and His character?

_____

_____

_____

Optional Application: In Ezekiel 9:4, the faithful ones who grieved over Jerusalem's detestable sins would receive God's mark of protection during the time of judgment. Use this passage to help you consider your own sensitivity to sin. In your own life, in your church, in your community, or in your nation — are there particular sins that cause you genuine grief and sorrow? Speak with God about this now.

For Thought and Discussion: What does Ezekiel 9:8 reveal about the deep concerns of Ezekiel's heart? And how would you compare Ezekiel's concerns here with God's concerns?

43

For Thought and Discussion: What could be the particular significance of the actions taken by "the man clothed in linen" in chapter 10?

Ezekiel 10

24. What does Ezekiel hear and see in 10:1-8?

_____

_____

_____

The glory of the LORD rose from above the cherubim and moved to the threshold of the temple. . . . Then the glory of the LORD departed from over the threshold (10:4,18). Recall also 9:3. "Ezekiel sees . . . the glory of God on the move once more, just as it had been in the days of the desert wanderings (see Exodus 40:34-37). It departs slowly, haltingly, as if reluctant to leave. . . . The city itself is now effectively doomed, cut off from the divine aid from its true protector. . . . The Lord has abandoned the city to the empty hope offered by the idols for which the people abandoned him."[11]

25. a. Describe as best you can what Ezekiel hears and sees in 10:9-17.

_____

_____

_____

b. How does this reinforce and build upon the impact of what Ezekiel saw in chapter 1?

_____

_____

_____

26. What happens in 10:18-19, and what is the significance of this?

_____

_____

_____

The glory of the LORD departed (10:18). "God's glory departed from the temple and was never completely present again until Christ himself visited it in New Testament times. God's holiness required that he leave the temple because the people had so defiled it. God had to completely destroy what people had perverted in order for true worship to be revived."[12]

27. In 10:15 and 10:20-22, Ezekiel specifically links this new vision with what he had seen in chapter 1. What significance do you see in this emphasis on Ezekiel's part?

_____

_____

_____

_____

28. What is revealed most about the Lord and His character in chapter 10?

_____

_____

_____

_____

29. What would you select as the key verse or passage in Ezekiel 4–10 — one that best captures or reflects the dynamics of what these chapters are all about?

_____

_____

For Thought and Discussion: Review the appearance and behavior of the cherubim in Ezekiel 10 (and in chapter 1, where they are spoken of as "living creatures"). What more do you learn about cherubim and their significance in these passages: Genesis 3:24; Exodus 25:18-22; 26:1,31; 36:8,35; 37:6-9; Numbers 7:89; 1 Samuel 4:4; 2 Samuel 6:2; 22:11; 1 Kings 6:23-35; 7:29-36; 8:6-7; 2 Kings 19:15; Psalm 80:1; 99:1; Isaiah 37:16; Ezekiel 41:17-25; Hebrews 9:5?

_____

_____

30. List any lingering questions you have about
    Ezekiel 4–10.

_____

_____

_____

_____

For the group

You may want to focus your discussion for lesson 2
especially on the following issues, themes, and concepts (all of them major overall themes in Ezekiel).
How are they further developed in chapters 4–10?

• God's glory and sovereignty
• The depth of human sinfulness
• The certainty, nature, and purpose of God's
  judgment against sin
• The nature of God's covenant relationship with
  His people
• The promise of mercy and hope for the future

    The following numbered questions in lesson 2
may stimulate your best and most helpful discussion: 1, 3, 6, 8, 10, 11, 14, 20, 23, 27, 28, 29, and 30.
    Look also at the questions in the margins
under the headings "For Thought and Discussion"
and "Optional Application."

1. Iain M. Duguid, *Ezekiel*, in *The NIV Application
   Commentary*, ed. Terry Muck (Grand Rapids, MI:
   Zondervan, 1999), 88.
2. Duguid, 88.
3. Ralph H. Alexander, *Ezekiel*, vol. 6 of *The Expositor's Bible
   Commentary*, ed. Frank E. Gaebelein (Grand Rapids, MI:
   Zondervan, 1986), 769.
4. Duguid, 91.
5. Duguid, 108.
6. Duguid, 110.
7. *ESV Study Bible*, introduction to Ezekiel: "Dates in
   Ezekiel."

8. Alexander Maclaren, *Ezekiel, Daniel, and the Minor Prophets*, vol. 7 of *Expositions of Holy Scripture* (Grand Rapids, MI: Eerdmans, 1942), 5–7.
9. Maclaren, 6.
10. Duguid, 133.
11. Duguid, 147–148.
12. *Life Application Bible*, various editions (Wheaton, IL: Tyndale, 1988 and later), at Ezekiel 10:18.

EZEKIEL 11–15

The Glory Gone

1. Read through Ezekiel 11–15 in one sitting. What overall impressions do you gain of the text?

_____

_____

_____

_____

Now begin your verse-by-verse study.

Ezekiel 11

2. a. What happens to Ezekiel in 11:1, and what does Ezekiel see?

_____

_____

_____

b. What does the Lord tell Ezekiel about this in 11:2-4?

_____

_____

_____

For Further Study:
The people's words in 11:3 about building houses echoes the letter Jeremiah sent to the exiles telling them to "build houses" and settle down in Babylon.[3] What else do you learn about this letter to the exiles in Jeremiah 29:1-23?

Twenty-five men (11:1). Elders. Probably not the sun-worshipers from 8:16.

Haven't our houses been recently rebuilt? (11:3). Or, "The time is not near to build houses" (ESV). If this is a question, as in the NIV, then it shows the people of Jerusalem feeling foolishly secure that their houses won't soon be destroyed again. If it's a statement, as in the ESV, then it shows fear and lack of trust in God.

This city is a pot, and we are the meat (11:3). If the phrase earlier in this verse about building houses is a question (as in the NIV), then this is a smug claim that in God's eyes the exiles are "discarded bones"[1] while those who haven't been exiled are the meat, the valued ones. If the earlier phrase is a statement (as in the ESV), then this one expresses fear: "we're cooked!"[2]

3. Review carefully the Spirit-inspired prophecy of 11:5-12.

   a. What does God say that Israel is guilty of?

   _____

   _____

   _____

   b. What punishment does He pronounce?

   _____

   _____

   _____

You have killed many people in this city (11:6). These are God's words to Israel. Earlier, as punishment for His people's sins, God had instructed His angelic executioners, "Defile the temple and fill the courts with the slain. Go!" (9:7); these angelic destroyers then "went out and began killing throughout the city." God holds the people accountable for those deaths because their sin brought on the judgment.

4. The "recognition formula" (which we observed throughout chapters 6 and 7) is repeated in 11:10. What does this repeated usage say about God's character and about His purpose in bringing severe discipline among His people?

_____

_____

_____

_____

For Thought and Discussion: What do you think it meant practically for God to be a "sanctuary" for His people (11:16)? And what does that mean practically for us today?

Alas, Sovereign LORD! Will you completely destroy the remnant of Israel? (11:13). This is just like Ezekiel's response in 9:8.

---

5. In the larger picture, what is the best answer to the question Ezekiel asks the Lord in 11:13?

_____

_____

_____

_____

6. What truth does God want His people in exile to remember, according to 11:14-16?

_____

_____

_____

_____

The people of Jerusalem have said . . . "They are far away from the LORD" (11:15). Those left in Judah look down on the exiles.

I have been a sanctuary for them in the countries where they have gone (11:16). The Lord has left His sanctuary in Jerusalem because

51

Optional Application: What do you see as the personal significance for you and your church of the promises given in 11:17-20?

For Further Study: A restoration to the Promised Land is God's promise to Israel in Ezekiel 11:17. Explore the biblical background and foundation for this in Genesis 12:1-3,7; 26:3; 35:12; Leviticus 26:40-45; Deuteronomy 30:1-10.

For Further Study: Compare the promises in Ezekiel 11:19 with what you see in Deuteronomy 30:6; Jeremiah 31:31-34; Joel 2:28-29; Zechariah 7:12.

idolatry defiled it (see 8:6), and He has gone somewhere else: to Babylon, to be a sanctuary for the faithful people there. God is always a sanctuary for those who are faithful to Him, no matter where they are.

7. Carefully list the specific promises God makes to His people in 11:17-20.

_____

_____

_____

_____

I will gather you . . . and bring you back . . . and I will give you back the land of Israel again (11:17). The first time in this book that God promises restoration. See also 11:20.

I will give them an undivided heart and put a new spirit in them; I will . . . give them a heart of flesh (11:19). This is further developed in 36:26-27. On one hand, God gives the new heart and spirit. On the other hand, He tells the people to "get a new heart and a new spirit" (18:31). Divine action and human action work together. Unless God performs heart surgery, we can't fix our own hearts and live according to His commands. But we can't just be passive; we have to choose His heart surgery through active faith in Christ and cooperation with the Holy Spirit.

An undivided heart (11:19). Unmixed commitment to God.

They will be my people, and I will be their God (11:20). The first time in Ezekiel that God calls them "my people."

8. In chapter 11, how do verses 17-20 answer Ezekiel's earlier outcry in verse 13?

_____

52

_____

_____

9. What significance do you see in God's warning in 11:21?

_____

_____

_____

10. What did Ezekiel see and experience in 11:22-25?

_____

_____

_____

11. What does Ezekiel 11 reveal most about God and His character?

_____

_____

_____

_____

Ezekiel 12

For Further Study: Compare the phrase in the last half of Ezekiel 11:20 with the promise God made in Exodus 6:7 just before He delivered His people out of Egyptian slavery. What does this reveal about God's long-term, big-picture goal in His relationship with His people?

For Thought and Discussion: For believers today, how do Jesus and the Holy Spirit make possible the fulfillment of these words in Ezekiel 11:20: "They will follow my decrees and be careful to keep my laws. They will be my people, and I will be their God"?

Optional Application: What does Ezekiel 11:17-20 reveal about what God desires to see in your own life?

For Thought and Discussion: In Ezekiel 12:2, God reminds His prophet that he lives among people who "have eyes to see but do not see and ears to hear but do not hear." To what extent is that also true of Christians in today's world?

For Further Study: Compare the rebelliousness of God's people that you read about in Ezekiel with what you see in these passages: Deuteronomy 9:7,24; 31:27; Psalm 78:40; Isaiah 6:9-10; 30:1,9; 65:2; Jeremiah 5:21-23; Daniel 9:5-9; Acts 7:51-52.

For Further Study: In the story of Zedekiah ("the prince" in Ezekiel 12:10,12), what are the most important elements seen in these passages: 2 Kings 25:2-7; 2 Chronicles 36:11-13; Jeremiah 39:2-7; 52:1-11?

The word of the LORD came to me (12:1). An introduction to "a new series of messages."[4]

The people's underlying objection in chapter 12: "If judgment was to come, it would not be in their lifetime, as Ezekiel had declared."[5]

12. a. From Ezekiel 12:1-7, summarize what Ezekiel did in obedience to God's instruction.

_____

_____

_____

  b. Summarize the explanation God gives for this in 12:8-13.

_____

_____

_____

As they watch (12:3). This or a similar phrase is repeated in each verse in 12:3-7. The elders have eyes but don't see. They watch what Ezekiel is doing, but they don't take it to heart.

Bring out your belongings packed for exile (12:4). The exiles know all too well what it looks like to pack for exile, because they did it six years ago.

The prince (12:10,12). Ezekiel's term for Zedekiah, who was reigning in Jerusalem as Judah's last king. Here he represents the people in their blindness.

13. The "recognition formula" is found again in verses 15, 16, and 20 of chapter 12. From the context of those verses, what will further Israel's recognition of the Lord?

_____

I will spare a few of them (12:16). In the Middle
East at that time, each nation had its patron
god. If that nation was defeated, people thought
its god was weak. So God would spare some
exiles so that they could testify to the nations
that they were defeated because of their own
sins, not His weakness. God cared what the
nations thought of Him not because of His ego
but for their sake. He cared that they might
come to know the only real God.

---

14. a. Summarize what God wants His people to
      understand about Himself in the message
      given in 12:21-28.

          _____

          _____

          _____

    b. What does He most want them to understand
      about their own future?

          _____

          _____

          _____

No more false visions (12:24). In chapter 13 Ezekiel will have a lot to say about the so-called
visions of falsely optimistic prophets.

***I the LORD will speak what I will, and it shall
be fulfilled. . . . I will fulfill whatever I say,
declares the Sovereign LORD. . . . Whatever I
say will be fulfilled*** (12:25,28). The differences
between the true and false prophets are (1) the
source of their prophecy, and (2) whether what
they say comes to pass. (2) proves (1).

Optional Application: Reflect on God's stated determination to fulfill His spoken word and His promises (see Ezekiel 12:25,28). Consider which of God's promises He might want you to remember most and be assured of their fulfillment. Express your thoughts to Him about this, in trust and gratitude.

15. What does Ezekiel 12 reveal most to us about God's character?

_____

_____

_____

_____

Ezekiel 13

The people's underlying objection in chapter 13 is that Ezekiel is only one of many prophets. Most prophets are promising hope and giving reasons for optimism. Ezekiel is a lone voice of negativity. Why should the people listen to him?[6]

16. a. What are the chief characteristics of false prophets that the Lord calls attention to in 13:1-16?

_____

_____

_____

 b. By contrast, what do these verses imply that God expects from His true prophets?

_____

_____

_____

Foolish (13:3). The word didn't mean lack of intelligence. It meant "spiritual and moral insensitivity,"[7] ignorance about how the world really works.

You have not gone up to the breaches in the wall to repair it (13:5). The covenant under the Law of Moses was like a wall protecting the people. Unfaithfulness was like something that knocked holes in the wall. The prophets' job was to repair those holes by calling the people back to faithful obedience. But the prophets weren't doing their job. They were ignoring the unfaithful behavior.

For Further Study: Compare what Ezekiel 13 records about the deceptive foolishness of the prophets with what you see in Jeremiah 23:16-22; 29:8-9.

17. a. Look again at 13:5. According to this verse, what did the prophets of Israel *fail to do*?

_____

_____

_____

b. Why do you think this was such a serious infraction, from God's perspective?

_____

_____

_____

c. If these prophets had instead actually done what God says here that they should have done, what actions might that have involved on their part? What would it have looked like?

_____

_____

_____

18. What specific kinds of judgment and punishment does God promise in 13:1-16 against the false prophets?

_____

_____

_____

_____

Optional Application: How does Ezekiel 13:5 relate to what needs to be done among God's people today? And what is your part in this?

For Thought and Discussion: Are there false prophets today? If so, how can we recognize them for who they really are?

For Further Study: What do we learn in these New Testament passages to help us guard against false prophets: 2 Corinthians 11:13-15; Galatians 1:6-9; Colossians 2:8-10; 1 Timothy 1:3-7; 4:1-3; 6:3-5; 2 Timothy 2:15-19; 3:1-9; 4:3-4; 2 Peter 2:1-3?

Whitewash (13:10). Instead of repairing the breaches in the covenant wall, the only wall that can protect the people, the false prophets have encouraged the exiles to build their own flimsy walls and plaster over them to look good.

19. a. In 13:17-23 the attention turns to women who are false prophets. What specific wrong-doing on their part does God condemn?

_____

_____

_____

b. What specific kinds of punishment does God promise to deal out to them?

_____

_____

_____

You have killed those who should not have died and have spared those who should not live (13:19). They may not have literally murdered people, but a watchman on the walls who fails to see threats and warn the citizens is guilty of their deaths (see 3:17-21; 33:1-9). By failing to warn wrongdoers to change their ways, the false prophets will be responsible when the wrongdoers are punished. Who knows if some might have repented if they had been properly warned?

You disheartened the righteous . . . you encouraged the wicked (13:22). When the wicked are told not to worry, the righteous feel like it's not worthwhile to bother doing right and the wicked are encouraged to do even worse.

20. Notice the recurrence in chapter 13 of the "recognition formula" (in verses 9, 14, 21, and 23).

In context here, what is it that will bring about the greater recognition of the Lord?

_____

_____

_____

_____

21. What does chapter 13 reveal about God's character?

_____

_____

_____

_____

Optional Application: Material prosperity can be a whitewash to cover spiritual bankruptcy. Some people even get obsessed with home renovation and decoration. Does the pursuit of material things distract you from pursuing and serving Christ? If so, how?

For Further Study: How does the caution about false prophets in Deuteronomy 13:1-5 relate to the teaching of Ezekiel 13?

Ezekiel 14

In chapter 14, Ezekiel responds to two objections from the people. First, the people think the leaders in Judah are "ultimately responsible. If there was to be any judgment, it would be on them, not the exiles." Second, if the exiles are in danger of judgment, they think they simply need to find a righteous man like Noah or Job to pray for them, and God will spare them because of the righteous man. [8]

22. What is the best answer to the question God asks in 14:3?

_____

_____

_____

_____

_____

Idols in their hearts (14:3). The exiles are no more righteous than the idolaters in Jerusalem. They may not be worshiping idols as flagrantly, but they have idols in their hearts. Even while they go through the motions of seeking guidance from a true prophet, their hearts are with the false promises of the prophets who use magic (see 13:20) and other detestable practices.

To recapture the hearts of the people of Israel (14:5). Or, "lay hold of the hearts of the house of Israel" (ESV). The Hebrew verb here is used of forceful seizure or conquest.[9] God has that kind of passion in His mission to recapture those who have been led astray into worshiping other things.

---

23. a. What dangers and harmful effects of idolatry are highlighted by God's words in 14:1-11?

_____

_____

_____

_____

b. What does God say must be done by those who are guilty of idolatry?

_____

_____

_____

c. What does God promise to do against those who are captive to idolatry?

_____

_____

_____

d. What does 14:11 reveal about God's heart and desire for His people?

_____

_____

_____

_____

For Thought and Discussion: Ezekiel 14 begins by exposing idolatry on the part of Israel's elders. What particular forms of idolatry are most dangerous for the leaders of God's people today?

I the LORD have enticed that prophet (14:9). Or, "I, the LORD, have deceived that prophet" (ESV). Although it's also true that these prophets are responsible for their choices, God has allowed them to be deceived. God is ultimately in control; the false prophets haven't somehow foiled His plans. See also 1 Kings 22:18-23.

The people of Israel will no longer stray from me (14:11). Not even Israel's sin will ultimately thwart God from dwelling with His people.[10]

24. What is the main message the Lord is giving His people in 14:12-20?

_____

_____

_____

_____

For Further Study: Ezekiel 14:14 refers to the righteousness of Noah, Daniel, and Job. What do you learn about their righteousness in these passages: Genesis 6:9; Job 1:1,8; 2:3; Daniel 6:4-5,22?

25. What is the Lord's message of hope for His people in 14:21-23?

_____

_____

_____

_____

_____

Yet there will be some survivors (14:22). The righteous men couldn't hope to save even their own sons and daughters by their righteousness (see 14:20), but surprisingly, because of His mercy, God will save some sons and daughters from the disaster. This will be sheer grace.

Optional Application: What helps you be the most aware of your own temptations to idolatry? Take a moment in prayer, renewing your commitment to the Lord to keep yourself from idols (as we're commanded in 1 John 5:21).

For Thought and Discussion: The concept of usefulness is a major theme of the parable presented in Ezekiel 15. How would you define *usefulness* as it relates to who we are and what we do in God's kingdom?

26. What does chapter 14 reveal about God's character?

_____

_____

_____

_____

Ezekiel 15

> The people's objection that underlies chapters 15–16 is that God would never judge His chosen people as harshly as Ezekiel predicts.

27. a. In the vine parable in 15:1-8, what major points are made about Israel and about God?

_____

_____

_____

_____

  b. In the use of the "recognition formula" in 15:7, what is it that brings about the increased recognition of the Lord?

_____

_____

_____

Given (15:6). The Lord has already given the useless vine wood to be burnt once: He allowed Judah to be defeated in 605 and 597 BC and allowed some of her people to go into exile. But that burning didn't do any good; the people are as useless as ever. Soon they will be almost completely burnt.

The vine's only worth is for bearing fruit. God's chosen people, likewise, were chosen to be fruitful, to bless the nations (see Genesis 12:1-3), not just to exist as parasites. Judah has consistently failed to bear the fruit of blessing the nations, so now she will be burnt.

The exiles still have a chance to be fruitful if they change their ways and become faithful to God. They could bless the nation where they are exiled. Instead of doubting God because of what He has let them suffer, they should be motivated to turn back to Him. Compare how Jesus uses the imagery of the vine in John 15:1-16.

For Further Study: Reflect on the fire imagery in the parable of the useless vine (see 15:1-8). How is it a purifying force? A destroying force? Search out these two themes in the following passages: Exodus 15:7; 1 Kings 8:51; Isaiah 1:25-26; 5:24; 48:10; Malachi 3:2-3.

28. What does chapter 15 reveal most regarding God's character?

_____

_____

_____

_____

29. What would you select as the key verse or passage in Ezekiel 11–15 — one that best captures or reflects the dynamics of what these chapters are all about?

_____

_____

_____

30. List any lingering questions you have about Ezekiel 11–15.

_____

For Further Study:
How does the vine
parable in Ezekiel
15 compare to these
passages that depict
God's people as a
vine or its branches,
or as a vineyard:
Psalm 80:8-16; Isaiah
5:1-7; 27:2-6; Jeremiah
2:21; Hosea 10:1; John
15:1-17?

For Further Study:
Compare the con-
cept of usefulness in
Ezekiel 15 with what
you see in verses
8-20 in Paul's letter to
Philemon. (The name
Onesimus in that pas-
sage means "useful.")

**Optional
Application:** With
Ezekiel 15 in mind,
how would you
describe your own
usefulness to God
and His kingdom?
Practically speaking,
how has Christ made
you useful?

_____

_____

_____

For the group

You may want to focus your discussion for lesson 3 especially on the following issues, themes, and concepts (all of them major overall themes in Ezekiel). How are they further developed in chapters 11–15?

- God's glory and sovereignty
- The depth of human sinfulness
- The certainty, nature, and purpose of God's judgment against sin
- The nature of God's covenant relationship with His people
- The promise of mercy and hope for the future

The following numbered questions in lesson 3 may stimulate your best and most helpful discussion: 1, 3, 5, 7, 11, 14, 15, 21, 22, 23, 24, 25, 26, 29, and 30.

Remember to look also at the "For Thought and Discussion" and "Optional Application" questions in the margins.

1. *NIV Study Bible* (Grand Rapids, MI: Zondervan, 1985), at Ezekiel 11:3.
2. *ESV Study Bible* (Wheaton, IL: Crossway, 2008), at Ezekiel 11:2-3.
3. Iain M. Duguid, *Ezekiel*, in *The NIV Application Commentary*, ed. Terry Muck (Grand Rapids, MI: Zondervan, 1999), 149.
4. Ralph H. Alexander, *Ezekiel*, vol. 6 of *The Expositor's Bible Commentary*, ed. Frank E. Gaebelein (Grand Rapids, MI: Zondervan, 1986), 795.
5. Alexander, 795.
6. Alexander, 795.
7. Alexander, 800.
8. Alexander, 795.
9. Alexander, 806
10. Duguid, 185.

EZEKIEL 16–19

Sin's Ugliness

1. Read through Ezekiel 16–19 in one sitting. What overall impressions do you gain of the text?

   _____

   _____

   _____

   _____

2. Proverbs 2:1-5 tells about the sincere person who truly longs for wisdom and understanding and who searches the Scriptures for it—as if there were treasure buried there. Such a person will come to understand the fear of the Lord and discover the knowledge of God. As you continue exploring Ezekiel, what "buried treasure" would you like God to help you find here—to show you what God and His wisdom are really like? If you have this desire, express it as a prayer to God.

   _____

   _____

   _____

Now begin your verse-by-verse study.

Ezekiel 16

Ezekiel 16 is the book's longest message and its most shocking. Ezekiel uses graphic violence and explicit sexual imagery to shatter the exiles' fantasy of a holy Jerusalem. Translations tend to tone down the sexual language, but Ezekiel chooses the strongest possible terms for condemning Jerusalem as a prostitute. Sin isn't polite, and Ezekiel feels no pressure to be polite about it. The exiles need to wake up and face the ugly truth.

3. In 16:1-2, what purpose is stated by the Lord for the story He unfolds in this chapter?

_____

_____

_____

_____

Your ancestry and birth were in the land of the Canaanites; your father was an Amorite and your mother a Hittite (16:3). The city of Jerusalem already existed when the Hebrews first arrived in the land of Canaan. "Amorite" and "Hittite" are two of the people groups that occupied this area before the Hebrews came (see Genesis 10:16; 15:16; Numbers 13:29; Joshua 1:4; 5:1; 7:7; 24:15,18; Amos 2:10).

4. As the story unfolds, restate in your own words what happens in each of these sections:

16:3-5

_____

_____

_____

16:6-7

_____

_____

_____

16:8-14

_____

_____

_____

I passed by and saw you kicking about in your blood (16:6). Abandoning unwanted children — particularly girls — was extremely common in the ancient world. The infant was left out in the elements to die.

I said to you, "Live!" (16:6). Jerusalem was a depraved pagan city when God sent the young King David to conquer it and make it the capital city of his newly united nation and the future home of God's temple.

I gave you my solemn oath and entered into a covenant with you (16:8). In the ancient world, someone might rescue an abandoned baby girl to raise her as a prostitute, but it was rare for such a girl to be adopted as a daughter, and to want her as a bride was unimaginable. To lavish her with care and wealth was unthinkable. Ezekiel's hearers would know this was true grace.[1] Jerusalem did nothing to deserve becoming the place of God's throne.

---

5. As the story in chapter 16 continues, summarize what happens and what the Lord emphasizes in each of these sections:

16:15-22

_____

_____

For Further Study: For further background on the marriage imagery used in Ezekiel 16:8-14, explore these passages: Genesis 24:53; Ruth 3:9; Psalm 45:13-15; 132:13-17; Proverbs 2:17; Isaiah 61:10; Malachi 2:14.

For Thought and Discussion: In what ways does Ezekiel 16:3-14 accurately reflect what God has done for us through Christ?

Optional Application: Respond in grateful prayer to the Lord for the ways in which Ezekiel 16:3-14 portrays what He has already done for you.

16:23-29

_____

_____

_____

16:30-34

_____

_____

_____

Prostitute (16:15). "You . . . played the whore" (ESV). An earlier prophet, Hosea, had compared Israel's idolatry to the adultery of a wife who gives her husband's wealth to her lovers (see Hosea 2:4-14). Ezekiel takes this image and makes the degradation much more graphic.[2] There's no nice way to talk about what we're doing when we turn from the Lord to other religions or other things to make us happy.

Your favors . . . your beauty (16:15). Jerusalem forgot that everything she had was God's gift. She loved His gifts but not Him.

You adulterous wife! (16:32). In Ezekiel's world, a wife wasn't free to leave her husband for another man. That was appalling behavior. His metaphor doesn't work if we impose on it modern notions of women's rights and self-fulfillment. When we think about what we owe God, we need to see this wife's ingratitude through ancient eyes. Only then will we understand why God — Jerusalem's husband — had the right to take back everything He'd given her. For Ezekiel, changing religions isn't a matter of freedom to exercise one's personal preferences. It's a horrible betrayal.

Prefer strangers (16:32). Judah had long turned to other nations like Egypt, rather than to God, for national security.

6. What action does the Lord promise to take against His people in 16:35-41?

_____

_____

_____

7. State in your own words the summary the Lord gives in 16:42-43.

_____

_____

_____

Your older sister was Samaria . . . and your younger sister . . . was Sodom (16:46). Ezekiel compares Jerusalem to two other cities that were notoriously sinful in his hearer's minds. Sodom was destroyed for its crimes in the time of Abraham (see Genesis 18:20-21; 19:1-15). Samaria was destroyed for its sins about 130 years before Ezekiel's message. The exiles would think that both Samaria and Sodom deserved what they got. Ezekiel's point is that Jerusalem is worse — this would shock his hearers.

---

8. New elements are added to the story beginning in 16:44. Summarize the main points that the Lord makes in 16:44-52.

_____

_____

_____

_____

_____

Be ashamed and bear your disgrace (16:52). Ezekiel wants the people to feel shame that they are behaving like Sodom and Samaria. Good shame leads to repentance.

For Further Study: Ezekiel 16:20-21 refers to Israel's despicable practice of child-sacrifice. What do you learn about this abomination in these passages: 2 Kings 16:3; 21:6; Jeremiah 7:31; 19:5; 32:35?

Optional Application: "You did not remember," God says to His people (16:22). What does the Lord most want you to remember in what He has done for you in the past, both during your lifetime and before? Express this as a prayer of remembrance to Him.

For Further Study: Explore Judah's history of seeking security through foreign alliances (instead of by trusting in the Lord) in these passages: 2 Kings 16:7-8; 20:12-19; Jeremiah 2:36-37; Ezekiel 17:15.

For Further Study:
Explore the sins of Sodom and Samaria. *For Sodom:* Genesis 13:10,13; 18:20; 19:4-5; Ezekiel 16:49. *For Samaria:* 1 Kings 12:25-33; 15:30; 16:15-20,25-26,30-34. Observe also the comparisons of Jerusalem with Sodom in Isaiah 3:9, Jeremiah 23:14, and Lamentations 4:6. How do these passages add to your understanding of Ezekiel 16?

For Further Study:
To better understand the "everlasting covenant" mentioned in Ezekiel 16:60, what do you discover in these passages: Psalm 105:8; Isaiah 55:3; 61:8-9; Jeremiah 32:40; 50:5; Ezekiel 37:26-27; Hosea 2:19-20; Luke 1:72; Hebrews 13:20?

9. What does the Lord promise to do in 16:53-58 and for what reasons?

_____

_____

_____

_____

10. What is the Lord's promise to His people in 16:59-63, and what is its stated purpose?

_____

_____

_____

_____

I will remember the covenant I made with you (16:60). Man's unfaithfulness doesn't prevent God's faithfulness (see 2 Timothy 2:13).

And I will establish an everlasting covenant with you (16:60). God Himself will pay for the city's sins and establish a new covenant with a holy Jerusalem.

Jerusalem didn't deserve it the first time God chose her, in the time of King David. She won't deserve it the next time, when God restores her and chooses her again. She doesn't at all deserve a second chance, but God will give her one so that she can demonstrate to the nations His vast mercy toward the worst sinners.

You will remember your ways (16:61). She will remember her past crimes, not to wallow in shame, but as a motivation to show gratitude for mercy. She will know that her confidence is in God's goodness, not in her own deserving.[3]

---

11. The "recognition formula" occurs again in 16:62. What causes the increased recognition, and what does it lead to?

_____

_____

_____

When I make atonement for you (16:63). This will be done through Jesus Christ's death on the cross.

12. What does chapter 16 reveal most about the Lord and His character?

_____

_____

_____

_____

Ezekiel 17

Again Ezekiel is responding to an objection the exiles have. This time the objection is that it's unfair for God to punish people for their ancestors' sins. Ezekiel makes clear that the judgment about to fall on Judah is for this generation's own sins, not those of their parents' generation.

He uses the form of a story that is part fable and part riddle about the political situation in Judah.

13. Summarize the main elements in the parable the Lord asks Ezekiel to tell in 17:1-10.

_____

_____

_____

_____

For Further Study:
What do you learn from how the eagle is used symbolically in earlier Old Testament passages? See Deuteronomy 28:49; Isaiah 46:11; Jeremiah 48:40; 49:22.

For Thought and Discussion: Consider how Ezekiel 17 confirms God's involvement in the great events of that day. If a parable were told about God's involvement in the great events of our day, what might it include?

A great eagle (17:3). Nebuchadnezzar, king of Babylon. The cedar sprig is King Jehoiachin of Judah, exiled to Babylon at the same time as Ezekiel.

One of the seedlings of the land (17:5). Zedekiah, the current king of Judah, installed by Nebuchadnezzar in Jehoiachin's place.

Another great eagle (17:7). Egypt. Zedekiah was seeking Egypt's help to free himself from Babylon's control. Zedekiah's rebellion against his lord, Nebuchadnezzar, echoes Judah's rebellion against her Lord, God.[4]

14. What explanation for the parable does the Lord give in 17:11-15? Summarize this in your own words.

_____

_____

_____

_____

15. What does the Lord promise to do in 17:16-21?

_____

_____

_____

16. What circumstances are linked with the "recognition formula" in 17:21?

_____

_____

_____

17. a. What does the Lord promise to do in 17:22-24 and for what purpose?

_____

_____

b. In this passage, what circumstances are linked with the "recognition formula" in 17:24, and why is this significant?

_____

_____

_____

For Further Study: Consider again the imagery used and the promises conveyed in 17:22-24. What connection is there with the messianic implications you find in these passages: Isaiah 11:1; Jeremiah 23:5-6; 33:14-16; Zechariah 3:8; 6:12-13?

Optional Application: What personal encouragement do you find in Ezekiel 17:24? How can you relate God's words here to your own circumstances?

I myself (17:22). Even though all of the kings of David's line have failed to keep the covenant and rule the true kingdom of God, God Himself will be faithful to His promises to David. A sprig from the tree of David — a king from his line — will surpass all the past kings and will have a worldwide influence.

I will break off a tender sprig (17:22). This sprig will not be from the line of Jehoiachin, because Jeremiah 22:28-30 said the throne would be taken away from that line. This sprig will be from other descendants of David.[5]

I the LORD have spoken, and I will do it (17:24). See also 22:14, 36:36, and 37:14. "Yahweh is by definition a God who acts. . . . Knowledge of his person and character is gained by observing his performance."[6]

18. What does chapter 17 reveal most about God's character?

_____

_____

_____

_____

73

For Further Study:
How would you com-
pare Ezekiel 18:1-4
with what the Lord
declares through the
prophet Jeremiah in
Jeremiah 31:27-30?

For Further Study:
Think about the kinds
of behavior and char-
acter qualities com-
mended in Ezekiel
18:5-18. This passage
shows that a person's
treatment of other
people reveals his
or her true attitude
toward God. How
does this passage
compare with what
is taught in Psalms 15
and 24?

**For Thought and
Discussion:** How
do the behavior
and character quali-
ties commended
in Ezekiel 18:5-18
compare with what
God desires in the
behavior of Christians
today?

**Optional
Application:** How
do the behavior
and character quali-
ties commended in
Ezekiel 18:5-18 com-
pare with what God
is working to bring
about in your life at
this time?

Ezekiel 18

In chapter 18, the exiles' underlying objection
is that their own repentance would make no
difference to any coming judgment, because
(they still insist) their parents' sins are the ones
being judged. They are still blind to their own
wrongdoing.

The exiles misunderstand Exodus 20:5,
where God says He visits the sins of the
fathers on the children. They incorrectly
believe God means that He punishes the
children for the fathers' sins. But what God
really means is that the parent's sin affects the
child. Parents model right and wrong for their
children. Children repeat what they see their
parents do. This is tragic, but each generation
is still responsible for its actions. Each child
has the chance to break the cycle. The exiles
have failed to break the cycle of sin, and they
are responsible for that.

19. What fact does the Lord affirm in 18:1-4, and
    what prompts this affirmation?

    _____

    _____

    _____

20. In 18:5-29, determine the main point made by
    the Lord in each of the following sections and
    express it in your own words:

    18:5-9

    _____

    _____

    18:10-13

    _____

    _____

18:14-20

_____

_____

_____

_____

18:21-29

_____

_____

_____

For Further Study:
Compare the message of Ezekiel 18 with what you see in these passages: Leviticus 18:1-5; Deuteronomy 11; 26:16-19; 30:15-20. How do these passages deepen your understanding of Ezekiel 18?

For Further Study:
Reflect deeply on God's words in Ezekiel 18:23 about the delight He experiences when a wicked person turns to Him in obedience and thereby gains life. Consider also His strong words in 18:32: "I take no pleasure in the death of anyone, declares the Sovereign LORD." In the New Testament, how is this truth reflected and reinforced in the words of 2 Peter 3:9?

Suppose there is a righteous man. . . . Suppose he has a violent son. . . . But suppose this son has a son who sees all the sins his father commits, and . . . he does not do such things (18:5,10,14). The exiles know that this exact pattern was played out by the godly King Hezekiah; his wicked son, Manasseh; and his godly great-grandson, Josiah.[7]

The one who sins is the one who will die (18:20). The exiles are in part suffering for the sins of earlier generations. But they are also guilty of similar sins, and they need to take responsibility for their own faults. They need to stop blaming others — their parents and God — for their predicament.

If a wicked person turns away from all the sins they have committed . . . that person will surely live; they will not die (18:21). God is eager to forgive the sins of the past if the wicked person will only turn away from rebellion.

21. What do you see as the significance of God's words in 18:23?

_____

_____

For Thought and Discussion: With Ezekiel 18:25 in mind, to what extent do you ever feel that God is unfair in lavishing His grace upon repentant sinners whose misdeeds are particularly repugnant to you?

For Further Study: Review the biblical principles of individual responsibility as revealed in these passages: Genesis 2:17; 4:7; Deuteronomy 24:16; 2 Kings 14:6. Recall also Ezekiel 3:16-21 and 14:12-20.

But if a righteous person turns from their righteousness and commits sin (18:24). Not even a person who is righteous because of trusting in Christ is free to sin without consequences.

The way of the Lord is not just (18:25,29). The exiles are blind to the many injustices they themselves commit, so they are quick to blame God for not treating them like righteous people.

22. What does the Lord ask His people to do in 18:30-32 and for what reasons?

_____

_____

_____

23. In what ways does God's teaching in 18:31 connect with what He said previously in Ezekiel 11:19?

_____

_____

_____

24. What principles of moral responsibility do you see in chapter 18?

_____

_____

_____

_____

25. What does chapter 18 reveal about God's character?

_____

_____

_____

Ezekiel 19

The people's underlying objection in chapter 19 is that King Zedekiah can be trusted to break free of Babylon with Egypt's help.

26. a. In chapter 19, what is indicated in the opening phrase as well as the final phrase about the nature of the content in this chapter?

_____

_____

_____

_____

b. How should that affect our interpretation of chapter 19?

_____

_____

_____

_____

A lioness (19:2). Israel. The lions are the other nations.

One of her cubs . . . became a strong lion (19:3). The cubs are recent kings of Judah. The strong lion here is King Jehoahaz, who was taken captive to Egypt (see 2 Kings 23:31-34; 2 Chronicles 36:1-4; Jeremiah 22:10-12).

Another of her cubs . . . a strong lion (19:5). Jehoiachin, the son of Jehoahaz, taken captive to Babylon (see 2 Kings 24:8-17; 25:27-30; 2 Chronicles 36:8-10).

For Further Study: With Ezekiel's story of the lions in mind (see 19:1-9), what do you discover from the figurative use of a lion in these passages as well: Genesis 49:9; Numbers 23:24; 1 Kings 10:19-20; Micah 5:8; Revelation 5:5?

27. From 19:2-9, summarize what happens in the first part of this poem of lament.

_____

_____

_____

28. From 19:10-14, summarize what happens in the final part of this poem of lament.

_____

_____

_____

Fire spread from one of its main branches and consumed its fruit (19:14). The devastation that Judah's current king is bringing on the nation by his rebellion against Babylon.

29. What would you select as the key verse or passage in Ezekiel 16–19 — one that best captures or reflects the dynamics of what these chapters are all about?

_____

_____

_____

30. List any lingering questions you have about Ezekiel 16–19.

_____

_____

_____

_____

78

For the group

You may want to focus your discussion for lesson 4 especially on the following issues, themes, and concepts (all of them major overall themes in Ezekiel). How are they further developed in chapters 16–19?

- God's glory and sovereignty
- The depth of human sinfulness
- The certainty, nature, and purpose of God's judgment against sin
- The nature of God's covenant relationship with His people
- The promise of mercy and hope for the future

The following numbered questions in lesson 4 may stimulate your best and most helpful discussion: 1, 12, 13, 18, 21, 24, 25, 29, and 30.

Remember to look also at the "For Thought and Discussion" and "Optional Application" questions in the margins.

1. Iain M. Duguid, *Ezekiel*, in *The NIV Application Commentary*, ed. Terry Muck (Grand Rapids, MI: Zondervan, 1999), 216.
2. Duguid, 211.
3. Duguid, 214-215.
4. Duguid, 224.
5. Ralph H. Alexander, *Ezekiel*, vol. 6 of *The Expositor's Bible Commentary*, ed. Frank E. Gaebelein (Grand Rapids, MI: Zondervan, 1986), 822.
6. Daniel I. Block, *The Book of Ezekiel: Chapters 1-24*, in the *New International Commentary on the Old Testament* (Grand Rapids, MI: Eerdmans, 1997), 50.
7. Alexander, 825.

EZEKIEL 20–24

Rebellion, Idolatry, and Judgment

1. Read through Ezekiel 20–24 in one sitting. What overall impressions do you gain of the text?

_____

_____

_____

_____

Now begin your verse-by-verse study.

Ezekiel 20

In the seventh year, in the fifth month on the tenth day (20:1). August 591 BC.[1]

2. For setting the scene in chapter 20, what are the most important elements in 20:1-4?

_____

_____

_____

Some of the elders . . . sat down in front of me
(20:1). As in the scenes in 8:1 and 14:1, the
elders come to ask Ezekiel for a prophecy. He
will refuse; he has told them plenty already, and
they have not responded well.

Have you come to inquire of me? (20:3). God
won't even let the elders get their request out of
their mouths. Having failed to repent by now,
they don't deserve His patience.

3. Summarize and outline the main features of
   Israel's national history that are given in each of
   the following sections of chapter 20.

   20:4-10

   _____

   _____

   _____

   20:11-17

   _____

   _____

   _____

   20:18-26

   _____

   _____

   _____

   20:27-31

   _____

   _____

   _____

Ezekiel's account of Israel's history in
20:4-31 puts a somewhat different light

on the exodus from Egypt than what we get in the books of Moses. There's no contradiction, but the things that are emphasized or left out are significant. First, God alone is leader; Moses and Joshua aren't mentioned. Second, the story focuses on Israel's time outside the Promised Land — a fitting emphasis for an audience of exiles. Third, no neighboring nations share the blame for tempting Israel to idolatry; the fault is wholly Israel's.[2] Fourth, Ezekiel focuses on the choices of three generations to obey or not to obey. They all disobey, and God's response of justice and mercy is a lesson not just for them but more importantly for the nations who are watching to see what God is like. The current generation (the exiles) should learn from what happened to their ancestors.

For Thought and Discussion: In the recounting of Israel's history in Ezekiel 20:4-29, in what ways, if any, do you see God's love coming through? In what ways do you see God's holiness coming through?

4. a. Read 20:4-31 again, and look for recurring patterns. What are the most significant concerns expressed here on God's part?

_____

_____

_____

b. What are the most prevalent attitudes and responses of God's people revealed here?

_____

_____

_____

83

c. What is revealed or implied about God's purposes for His people?

_____

_____

_____

d. Explain the significance of the "recognition formula" here as you see it in context in verses 12, 20, and 26.

_____

_____

_____

Of all the laws God gave Israel, Ezekiel focuses on the Sabbath (see 20:12,13,16,20,21,24). We are accustomed to a seven-day week, but in the ancient world it was a unique way of laying out sacred time. Pagan calendars followed the cycles of the moon and the seasons of nature and agriculture. Resting for one day out of seven was a powerful symbol of submission to a God who was Lord over agriculture and who could make sure that there was enough time to get the work done. "To profane the Sabbath was thus to abandon an essential element of their distinctiveness as the people of the Lord and to attempt, in effect, to 'become like the nations around us.'"[3]

The person who obeys them will live (20:13). This phrase is not an argument for eternal salvation by works. Obedience showed faith in God; disobedience showed unbelief. "Those who received life by faith in God were to live that life by keeping his commandments—then and now (see Romans 10:4-5; Galatians 3:10-25)."[4]

Other statutes that were not good (20:25). Laws and customs from the neighboring nations. The Israelites interpreted God's laws in light of these pagan customs. God "gave" these statutes in the sense that He allowed Israel to be exposed to them. He knew the people would choose to adopt them.

For Further Study: What do you learn about the Sabbath from Genesis 2:2-3; Exodus 16:29; 20:8-11; 31:13-17; Leviticus 23:3,24,32,39; 25:4; Deuteronomy 5:12-15; Nehemiah 9:14; Mark 2:27-28?

5. a. Compare 20:3 with 20:30-31. What does this say about the people's relationship with God?

_____

_____

_____

_____

For Further Study: Compare the Lord's words in Ezekiel 20:13 with the promise of life in Leviticus 18:5 and Deuteronomy 30:15-20. Compare also two passages in the New Testament —Romans 10:5-13 and Galatians 3:11-14 —in which Paul uses Leviticus 18:5 as a springboard into the gospel. Summarize how these passages relate to the gospel of Jesus Christ.

b. What does God then emphasize in 20:32?

_____

_____

_____

c. What is especially significant in God's assertions and His promises in 20:33-38?

_____

_____

_____

_____

d. What supreme concern on God's part is revealed in 20:39?

_____

_____

_____

For Further Study:
Review God's asser-
tion in Ezekiel 20:25
about giving over His
people to bad influ-
ences, and compare
this with the situation
described in Numbers
11:4-6,31-34. Compare
it also with what you
see in Acts 7:42 and
Romans 1:24,26,28.

**Optional
Application:** Review
God's promise to His
people in Ezekiel
20:41 to display His
glory among them.
Think about your
desire for this to hap-
pen in your own life
and in your church.
What might this look
like as God reveals His
glory among you and
through you? Pray to
this end.

_____

_____

To this day (20:31). This day is what Ezekiel cares
about. Today is like yesterday: "vile images,
child sacrifice, and idolatry."[5]

_____

6. What are the chief features in God's promises as
revealed in 20:40-44?

_____

_____

_____

Like the earlier generations, the current
generation deserves to be utterly destroyed. But as in the earlier times, God will
spare them because of His own merciful
character, because of His faithfulness to His
covenant promises, and because He cares
what the nations believe about Him.

_____

The word of the LORD came to me (20:45). In
Hebrew, this begins chapter 21.

_____

7. What message is given to Ezekiel in 20:45-48,
and who is it for?

_____

_____

_____

8. What do we learn about Ezekiel's reputation in
20:49?

_____

_____

Ezekiel 21

9. The *sword* is the key image of chapter 21. Describe how this theme is developed and the major points God makes in each of these sections:

21:1-5

_____

_____

21:8-13

_____

_____

21:14-17

_____

_____

21:18-27

_____

_____

21:28-32

_____

_____

_____

10. From its context here, what is the significance of the "recognition formula" in 21:5?

For Thought and Discussion: What is particularly appropriate about the Lord identifying Himself with the imagery of a sword, as He does in Ezekiel 21?

_____

_____

_____

11. What significance do you see in what the Lord tells Ezekiel to do and say in 21:6-7?

_____

_____

_____

He will cast lots with arrows, he will consult his idols, he will examine the liver (21:21). Ironically, these pagan ways of consulting the gods will tell the king the will of the true God.[6]

12. What are the key points given in 21:24-27, a passage centering on Israel's "prince"?

_____

_____

_____

You people have brought to mind your guilt (21:24). They haven't simply brought their guilt to their own awareness. They have made it public, as in a court of law, and are subject to justice.[7]

You profane and wicked prince of Israel (21:25). Zedekiah (see also 12:10,12).

Until he to whom it rightfully belongs shall come (21:27). There's a double meaning here. Immediately, the crown belongs to Nebuchadnezzar of Babylon, and he is about to come and claim it in judgment. Longer term, the crown belongs to the Messiah, and ultimately He will come to claim it.

I will judge you (21:30). Babylon is God's sword of judgment, but eventually God will also judge Babylon. God is judge of all the earth. Babylon will learn that it has triumphed not because its power is greater than God's, or because its gods are greater than God. Babylon will turn out to be merely a tool in God's hand, as dependent on God as Judah is.

Ezekiel 22

13. The shedding of blood is the key image and theme in chapter 22. Summarize the sins that are associated with this image in each of the following sections:

    22:1-5

    _____

    _____

    _____

    22:6-12

    _____

    _____

    _____

    22:13-16

    _____

    _____

    _____

14. In 22:17-22, what does the Lord communicate through the imagery of melting and refining metals?

    _____

    _____

    _____

For Further Study:
Review the story of King Zedekiah in 2 Kings 24:18–25:26.

Optional Application:
Passages like Ezekiel 21 and 22 are seldom anyone's favorite in Scripture, yet all parts of God's Word have their purpose and their intended, inescapable effect (recall Isaiah 55:10-11). In your own life and your relationship with God, what values and purposes are served most by Ezekiel 21 and 22?

For Further Study:
With Ezekiel 22:17-22
in mind, explore the
images of the fire of
refinement and the
fire of judgment in
the following pas-
sages: Isaiah 1:21-31;
48:10; Jeremiah 6:27-
30; Malachi 3:2-3.

For Further Study:
Compare the list of
sins in Ezekiel 22:25-
28 with the prophecy
in Zephaniah 3:3-4.
What links do you
see?

15. From its context here in chapter 22, what is the
    significance of the "recognition formula" as it
    occurs . . .

    in 22:16?

    _____

    _____

    _____

    in 22:22?

    _____

    _____

    _____

16. What is the main thrust of the Lord's message
    to Ezekiel in 22:23-29?

    _____

    _____

    _____

    _____

Stand before me in the gap (22:30). In 13:5, the
    prophet's task was to repair the broken places
    in the covenant wall. Here the prophet's task is
    simply to stand before God in the broken place,
    to beg God to have mercy on the sinful people.
    The prophet must face the pain that such
    prayer brings, and he even risks God's anger.
    Moses took this risk after Israel made a golden
    calf idol (see Psalm 106:23).

*Bringing down on their own heads all they have
    done, declares the Sovereign Lord* (22:31).
    This prophecy ends with the same menacing
    words that end the prediction of Jerusalem's
    destruction (chapters 9–11; see 11:21). The
    echo links the two messages together.

17. What is communicated in 22:30-31 regarding the Lord's intentions and purposes and His way of dealing with His people?

_____

_____

_____

For Thought and Discussion: What images or statements in Ezekiel 23 might have been most shocking when the prophet's words first came to the people, and why?

Ezekiel 23

Like chapter 16, this chapter compares Jerusalem to a prostitute. But while chapter 16 focused on Jerusalem's "spiritual adultery" with pagan religions, chapter 23 focuses on the city's "political adultery."[8] To get out from under Babylon's control, Jerusalem was seeking alliances with foreign nations rather than submitting to God. Samaria had done the same thing 130 years earlier when Assyria was the ascendant power. Once again, the sexual language is chosen deliberately to shock the hearers awake.

For Further Study: What do you discover about Israel's involvement with the Assyrians in these passages: 2 Kings 15:19-20; 17:3-4; Hosea 5:13; 7:11; 8:9; 12:1-2; Amos 5:26?

18. a. According to 23:1-4, who is represented by the sisters Oholah and Oholibah?

_____

_____

_____

_____

b. In what important ways are these two alike?

_____

_____

_____

_____

The older was named Oholah, and her sister was Oholibah (23:4). The similarity of the names implies that they are twins with the same character, "like Tweedledum and Tweedledee."[9]

19. Summarize Oholah's story as told in 23:5-10.

_____

_____

_____

_____

She became a byword (23:10). Literally, a "name."[10] Samaria's name became synonymous with political prostitution and well-deserved punishment. Most people from Judah would have readily agreed that Samaria deserved all she got. The idea that Jerusalem was cut from the same cloth would have been offensive. Ezekiel wants his hearers to learn from Samaria's mistakes and avoid her fate.

20. Summarize Oholibah's story as told in 23:11-21.

_____

_____

_____

_____

Then the Babylonians came to her. . . . She turned away from them in disgust (23:17). Jerusalem's current king, Zedekiah, was

Babylon's puppet in the beginning, but then he decided he wanted his independence. However, in turning away from Babylon, he didn't turn away from foreign political intrigue. He just looked for greener grass in other countries. He was still prostituting the nation with foreign powers instead of trusting God.

For Further Study: What do you discover about Judah's involvement with the Assyrians in these passages: 2 Kings 16:5-7; 20:12-19; Isaiah 7:1-2?

21. a. What does the Lord promise to do to Oholibah in 23:22-35?

_____

_____

_____

b. What reasons does the Lord give for treating Oholibah this way?

_____

_____

_____

Optional Application: In Ezekiel 23:35 the Lord tells His people, "You have forgotten me and turned your back on me." In what situations or circumstances are you most tempted to forget God? Have you done this recently? If you have, confess this to God, with new recognition for how hurtful this is to Him.

22. What wrongdoing by Oholah and Oholibah does the Lord point to in 23:36-45?

_____

_____

_____

23. a. What does the Lord promise to do against His people in 23:46-49?

_____

_____

_____

b. In this context, what is the significance of the "recognition formula" in 23:49?

_____

_____

Ezekiel 24

In the ninth year, in the tenth month on the tenth day (24:1). January 588 or 587 BC.[11] The catastrophe that Ezekiel has predicted for twenty-three chapters finally begins.

24. What important news does the Lord give Ezekiel in 24:1-2?

_____

_____

_____

Record this date, this very date (24:2). When Jerusalem is eventually destroyed, this date will be evidence that Ezekiel is a true prophet whose predictions come to pass.

This rebellious people (24:3). Ezekiel uses this phrase fourteen times. Judah's "rebellion against Nebuchadnezzar is not a glorious (if doomed) fight for freedom and self-determination but rather an expression of their basic rebellious nature—a rebellion fundamentally directed against God."[12]

Put on the cooking pot. . . . Put into it the pieces of meat (24:3-4). See the earlier use of this metaphor in 11:3.

25. a. In the message given to Ezekiel for God's people in 24:3-13, explain the imagery God uses and its meaning.

_____

_____

b. State in your own words the thrust of the Lord's concluding statements about this in 24:14.

_____

_____

_____

_____

For Further Study: Examine the concept of uncovered blood by studying these passages: Genesis 4:8-11; Leviticus 17:13; Numbers 35:33; Deuteronomy 12:16,24; Isaiah 26:21. How do they broaden your understanding of Ezekiel 24:7-8?

Blood . . . poured . . . on the bare rock. . . . I put her blood on the bare rock, so that it would not be covered (24:7-8). In Hebrew, to atone is literally to "cover." Just as sin had to be atoned for by blood sacrifice, so even blood that was shed for a legitimate reason (such as hunting for food) had to be drained out of the animal on the ground and covered with soil (see Leviticus 17:13). Blood left out uncovered was sacrilegious and invited God's wrath. Even more abominable was the kind of murderous bloodshed that Ezekiel talks about here. Jerusalem would suffer the same fate: the blood of her people would be shed and the bodies left unburied. This was felt to be a horrible fate.

For Thought and Discussion: What kind of reactions do you imagine were going through Ezekiel's mind when he first received the message God gave him in Ezekiel 24:15-17?

I the LORD have spoken. The time has come for me to act (24:14). Recall also 17:24 and 22:14.

26. a. Summarize what Ezekiel experiences in 24:15-18.

_____

_____

_____

b. What meaning and significance for this is unfolded in 24:19-24?

_____

_____

_____

With one blow (24:16). The death of Ezekiel's wife at the same time as the siege of Jerusalem (the death of God's bride) is the most painful sign-act he has to endure. His wife dies young (Ezekiel is thirty-five), and he is commanded not to mourn. He doesn't protest; he obeys without question. Mourning rituals are sacred in Jewish culture, so people are shocked when he ignores them (see 24:19). He is acting out what they will go through when their beloved city is destroyed.

You will not mourn or weep (24:23). The exiles will be so overwhelmed with grief that they won't be able to go through with the normal public mourning rites. They will be too appalled to cry. When a family member dies, neighbors are normally a source of support, but when the whole community is grief-stricken, no one will be able to reach out.

---

27. a. What does the Lord promise Ezekiel in 24:25-27, and in what circumstances?

_____

_____

_____

b. In this context, what is the significance of the "recognition formula" in 24:27?

_____

_____

_____

At that time your mouth will be opened; you will . . . no longer be silent (24:27). At the beginning of his ministry (see 3:26), Ezekiel was commanded to be mute. He was unable to pray

96

for Jerusalem; he could only speak of judgment. When Jerusalem is destroyed, he will no longer need to speak of judgment against her.

The first section of Ezekiel's book is ending. In chapters 25–32 he will speak of judgment against the surrounding nations, and when his muteness is ended (chapter 33), for the rest of the book he will offer hope of restoration.

Optional Application: Reflect on Ezekiel's experience with the loss of his wife in 24:15-18. Think about how reluctant Ezekiel would naturally be to obey God's words here and how difficult it would be for him. What are the most difficult things God has asked you to do? What can you learn from Ezekiel's example?

28. What do chapters 20–24 reveal most about the Lord and His character?

_____

_____

_____

_____

29. What would you select as the key verse or passage in Ezekiel 20–24 — one that best captures or reflects the dynamics of what these chapters are all about?

_____

_____

_____

_____

30. List any lingering questions you have about Ezekiel 20–24.

_____

_____

_____

_____

For the group

You may want to focus your discussion for lesson 5 especially on the following issues, themes, and concepts (all of them major overall themes in Ezekiel). How are they further developed in chapters 20–24?

- God's glory and sovereignty
- The depth of human sinfulness
- The certainty, nature, and purpose of God's judgment against sin
- The nature of God's covenant relationship with His people
- The promise of mercy and hope for the future

The following numbered questions in lesson 5 may stimulate your best and most helpful discussion: 1, 4, 6, 17, 28, 29, and 30.

Remember to look also at the "For Thought and Discussion" and "Optional Application" questions in the margins.

1. *ESV Study Bible* (Wheaton, IL: Crossway, 2008), introduction to Ezekiel: "Dates in Ezekiel."
2. ESV Study Bible, at Ezekiel 20:1-31.
3. Iain M. Duguid, *Ezekiel*, in *The NIV Application Commentary*, ed. Terry Muck (Grand Rapids, MI: Zondervan, 1999), 261.
4. Ralph H. Alexander, *Ezekiel*, vol. 6 of *The Expositor's Bible Commentary*, ed. Frank E. Gaebelein (Grand Rapids, MI: Zondervan, 1986), 835–836.
5. Duguid, 263.
6. Duguid, 276.
7. Duguid, 277.
8. Alexander, 851.
9. Duguid, 301.
10. Duguid, 302.
11. *ESV Study Bible*, introduction to Ezekiel: "Dates in Ezekiel."
12. Duguid, 313.

EZEKIEL 25–28

Oracles Against Israel's Neighbors

1. Read through Ezekiel 25–28 in one sitting. What overall impressions do you gain of the text?

_____

_____

_____

_____

Now begin your verse-by-verse study.

Ezekiel 25

At the moment when the besieging army is encircling Jerusalem, Ezekiel leaves the reader in suspense and changes his focus. We now get a series of messages against the surrounding nations. As in other prophetic books that contain messages against the nations, the point of these is to show that God is God of the whole world. He is not just some national

For Further Study: What do you learn in the similar predictions of judgment on the nations in Jeremiah 9:25-26; 25:15-27,31-33; 27:1-11?

For Thought and Discussion: In what specific ways does Ezekiel 25 affirm that the LORD is the one true God?

For Further Study:
What additional record do you see of God's judgment against Ammon in these passages: Jeremiah 49:1-6; Amos 1:13-15; Zephaniah 2:8-11?

deity. Israel is special to Him for the sake of blessing all nations, and all nations are subject to Him, whether for blessing or judgment.

The seven prophecies against the nations in chapters 25–29 move clockwise from Ammon (northeast of Judah) to Moab (east), Edom (southeast), Philistia (west), Tyre and Sidon (northwest), and finally back to the south for the climactic judgment against Judah's great enemy, Egypt.

Set your face against the Ammonites (25:2). Like many prophecies against foreign nations in the Old Testament, the one against the Ammonites shows God addressing the nation, states the nation's sinful attitudes and actions, and predicts the nation's downfall.[1]

2. a. Summarize the essential message in the prophecy against Ammon in 25:1-7.

_____

_____

_____

   b. How would you comment on this prophecy's link to the "recognition formula" in verses 5 and 7?

_____

_____

_____

3. How does 25:1-7 amplify and build upon Ezekiel's earlier words about Ammon in 21:20,28-32?

_____

_____

_____

For Further Study:
What additional
record do you see
of God's judgment
against Moab in
these passages: Isaiah
15–16; Jeremiah
48; Amos 2:1-3;
Zephaniah 2:8-11?

Judah has become like all the other nations
(25:8). There's a lot of truth in Moab's statement, and Ezekiel has said so. But on Moab's
lips the statement implies, "Judah was never a
chosen nation, and her God is just like all the
other gods." That's blasphemy, and God will
prove it wrong.

For Further Study:
What details of
Israel's troubled his-
tory with Edom do
you discover in these
passages: Genesis
25:22-34; 27:41-46;
32–33; 36; Numbers
20:14-21; 24:15-19;
Deuteronomy 23:7-8;
1 Samuel 14:47;
2 Samuel 8:14; 1 Kings
11:14-22; 2 Kings
8:20-22; 2 Chronicles
20:1-23; 28:17; Psalm
137:7; Lamentations
4:21-22; Ezekiel 36:1-7?

4. a. Summarize the essential message in the
prophecy against Moab in 25:8-11.

_____

_____

_____

b. How would you comment on this prophecy's
link to the "recognition formula" in verse 11?

_____

_____

_____

Edom took revenge on Judah (25:12). The prophet
Obadiah charges Edom with helping the Babylonians conquer Judah, then plundering Judah
and killing or handing over the refugees.

5. a. Summarize the essential message in the
prophecy against Edom in 25:12-14.

_____

_____

_____

b. Notice the variation of the "recognition formula" in verse 14. What significance do you see in this?

_____

_____

_____

6. a. Summarize the essential message in the prophecy against Philistia in 25:15-17.

_____

_____

_____

b. How would you comment on this prophecy's link to the "recognition formula" in verse 17?

_____

_____

_____

Ezekiel 26

Ezekiel devotes three chapters to three long prophecies against Tyre. Each one ends with the same doom: Tyre will have "a horrible end" and "will be no more" (26:21; 27:36; 28:19). These are not three separate messages but three movements presenting the same message in different ways.[2]

In the eleventh month of the twelfth year, on the first day of the month (26:1). Around 587-586 BC.[3]

7. a. Summarize the essential message in the prophecy against Tyre in 26:1-6.

_____

_____

_____

b. How would you comment on this prophecy's link to the "recognition formula" in verse 6?

_____

_____

_____

The gate to the nations is broken (26:2). The other foreign nations are condemned for opposing God's people. Tyre tried to set herself up as a replacement for Jerusalem, God's city. She thought the holy city's destruction was a chance for Tyre to become the center of the world, the gate to the nations.[4]

I will bring many nations against you, like the sea casting up its waves (26:3). The picture of waves on a stormy sea is appropriate for Tyre, because the city owed her strength to being built on a small island. The sea protected her from siege armies. It took the Babylonians thirteen years to subdue Tyre. She won her freedom again for a while, and then Persia conquered her. She collapsed after resisting Alexander the Great, then faced Antiochus III, then Rome, then finally Muslim conquerors in the fourteenth century AD.[5]

8. Describe the further judgments against Tyre as prophesied in these passages:

26:7-14

_____

_____

_____

For Further Study:
What additional record do you see of God's judgment against Edom in these passages: Isaiah 34:5-15; Jeremiah 49:7-22; Amos 1:11-12; Obadiah; Malachi 1:2-5?

For Further Study:
What details of Israel's troubled history with the Philistines do you discover in these passages: Judges 13–16; 1 Samuel 4; 13; 31; 2 Samuel 5; 2 Kings 18:8; 2 Chronicles 21:16-17; 28:18?

For Further Study:
What additional record do you see of God's judgment against Philistia in these passages: Isaiah 14:28-32; Jeremiah 47; Joel 3:4-8; Amos 1:6-8; Zephaniah 2:4-7?

For Further Study:
How did Tyre figure into Christ's ministry, according to these passages: Mark 7:24-31; Luke 6:17; 10:13-14?

For Further Study:
What additional
record do you see
of God's judgment
against Tyre in these
passages: Isaiah 23;
Joel 3:4-8; Amos
1:9-10?

26:15-21

_____

_____

_____

_____

You were a power on the seas (26:17). Tyre was a merchant power and established colonies around the Mediterranean Sea, along the Red Sea, and as far as the Indian Ocean.[6]

When I bring the ocean depths over you and its vast waters cover you (26:19). The Jews were not a seagoing people, and the ocean represented for them the mythological forces of chaos arrayed against the forces of order.[7]

To the pit . . . in the earth below (26:20). "The pit" was the abode of the dead apart from God. Bodies were commonly buried in large pits.[8]

You will not return or take your place in the land of the living (26:20). Or, "you will not be inhabited; but I will set beauty in the land of the living" (ESV); or, "you may never be inhabited; and I shall establish glory in the land of the living" (NKJV).

Ezekiel 27

Chapter 27 prophesies the same basic message as chapter 26 in the form of a lament, a funeral song.

9. Describe the characteristics and accomplishments of Tyre as featured in each of these sections:

27:1-7

_____

27:8-11 _____

_____

_____

27:12-17 _____

_____

_____

27:18-25 _____

_____

_____

For Further Study:
"I am perfect in beauty"—this was Tyre's boastful self-view (27:3). See also 28:2: "your heart is proud" (ESV). Summarize what the LORD says about such pride in these passages: Psalm 10:4; Proverbs 8:13; 16:5,18.

For Thought and Discussion: What present-day cities or nations would you say might be most similar to Tyre, according to the description given in Ezekiel 27:4-25?

10. a. What experience of tragedy for Tyre is revealed in 27:26-27?

_____

_____

b. What is the response to this tragedy in 27:28-36?

_____

_____

_____

Ezekiel 28

Chapter 28 repeats the message against Tyre for the third time, part prophecy

Optional Application: Think about how the oracles directed to Tyre (see Ezekiel 26–28) speak clearly against pridefulness (note especially 28:2). What particular temptations to pride does God most want you to be aware of and on guard against? Once you've identified these, ask for His help in this.

For Thought and Discussion: What phrases in Ezekiel 28 indicate the possibility that Satan, as well as the king of Tyre, may be in view?

and part lament for the king of Tyre, who represents his city. Ezekiel rhapsodizes about Tyre's splendor in order to emphasize how far she will fall.[9]

11. What characteristics of the prince of Tyre are highlighted in 28:1-5?

_____

_____

_____

12. What judgment against the prince of Tyre is pronounced in 28:6-10?

_____

_____

_____

The most ruthless of nations (28:7). Babylon. Used also in Ezekiel 31:12.

The death of the uncircumcised (28:10). A shameful death from a Jewish point of view.

13. What characteristics of the prince of Tyre are highlighted in 28:11-14?

_____

_____

_____

You were the seal of perfection, full of wisdom and perfect in beauty (28:12). At a literal level, this is a funeral song for the king of Tyre. With some sarcasm, the eulogy says the over-the-top things that the king would want said about himself.

106

You were in Eden, the garden of God; every pre-
cious stone adorned you (28:13). All of this
could be said in the king's eulogy. "God" could
refer to a god. "Eden" could represent some
paradise-like place. But many interpreters see
the lament shifting to a eulogy for Satan, who
was indeed in Eden (see Genesis 3). If the passage is about the king of Tyre, these claims
show him setting himself up as greater than
Adam, and destined for a fall like Adam's and
banishment from paradise.[10]

A guardian cherub (28:14). The word for "cherub"
can also refer to a sphinx. So if the passage is
not about Satan, then the king of Tyre claimed
to be the guardian sphinx of Tyre's chief god.
"The Phoenician male-sphinx (or cherub) was
normally bejeweled and sometimes had the
head of the priest-king. The sphinx was con-
sidered to be all-wise." The trouble with interpreting the passage as a description of Satan is
that nowhere else in Scripture are we told that
Satan wore jewels or was a guardian cherub in
Eden.[11]

Holy mount of God (28:14). In Canaanite mythology, "the mount of god" was the seat of the
gods in the far north. The king of Tyre claimed
to be a god. Nowhere in Scripture is "the
mount of God" used to refer to heaven.[12]

For Thought and Discussion: What do the final three verses in Ezekiel 28 demon-strate about God's desire for His people, then and now?

14. According to 28:15-19, what happened to the prince of Tyre and for what reasons?

_____

_____

_____

15. a. Summarize the essential message in the prophecy against Sidon in 28:20-24.

_____

_____

_____

b. How would you comment on this prophecy's link to the "recognition formula" in verses 23 and 24?

_____

_____

_____

No longer will the people of Israel have malicious neighbors (28:24). A summary of the prophecies in chapters 25–28.

16. What are the main features of the prophecy concerning Israel in 28:25-26, and what is its connection to the "recognition formula"?

_____

_____

_____

17. What do chapters 25–28 reveal most about the character of God?

_____

_____

_____

_____

18. Look back at the identical phrase that's found in the opening verse of chapters 25, 26, 27, and 28, and also in 28:11 and 28:20. What significance are we meant to recognize in this particular phrasing?

_____

_____

_____

_____

19. What would you select as the key verse or passage in Ezekiel 25–28 — one that best captures or reflects the dynamics of what these chapters are all about?

_____

_____

_____

20. List any lingering questions you have about Ezekiel 25–28.

_____

_____

_____

_____

For the group

You may want to focus your discussion for lesson 6 especially on the following issues, themes, and concepts (all of them major overall themes in Ezekiel). How are they further developed in chapters 25–28?

- God's glory and sovereignty
- The depth of human sinfulness
- The certainty, nature, and purpose of God's judgment against sin
- The nature of God's covenant relationship with His people
- The promise of mercy and hope for the future

The following numbered questions in lesson 6 may stimulate your best and most helpful discussion: 1, 15, 16, 17, 18, 19, and 20.

Once more, look also at the questions in the margins under the headings "For Thought and Discussion" and "Optional Application."

1. Iain M. Duguid, *Ezekiel*, in *The NIV Application Commentary*, ed. Terry Muck (Grand Rapids, MI: Zondervan, 1999), 323.
2. Duguid, 333.
3. *ESV Study Bible* (Wheaton, IL: Crossway, 2008),

introduction to Ezekiel: "Dates in Ezekiel."
4. Duguid, 336.
5. Ralph H. Alexander, *Ezekiel*, vol. 6 of *The Expositor's Bible Commentary*, ed. Frank E. Gaebelein (Grand Rapids, MI: Zondervan, 1986), 870.
6. Alexander, 869–870.
7. Duguid, 337.
8. Alexander, 903.
9. Duguid, 344, 347.
10. Alexander, 882–883; Duguid, 346.
11. Alexander, 883.
12. Alexander, 883–884.

EZEKIEL 29–32

Oracles Against Egypt

1. Read through Ezekiel 29–32 in one sitting. What overall impressions do you gain of the text?

   _____

   _____

   _____

   _____

   Now begin your verse-by-verse study.

Ezekiel 29

2. The opening verse of this chapter includes another repetition (the seventh occurrence) of the phrase seen earlier in 25:1, 26:1, 27:1, and 28:1,11,20. How do God's words against Egypt relate to those earlier oracles against various nations around Israel?

   _____

   _____

   _____

   _____

We have had four short oracles against Judah's neighbors, then a long prophecy against Tyre, and then a short one against Sidon. Seven was the Hebrew number of completion, and oracle number seven is directed against Egypt. Egypt was the old enemy where Israel was enslaved for centuries, but Egypt was also the rich neighbor who at times looked like a good ally against Babylon. Egypt encouraged Judah to rebel against Babylon, and when Babylon responded by besieging Jerusalem, Egypt made only a halfhearted attempt to break the siege. Egypt was never going to put herself at risk for Judah's sake.

In the tenth year, in the tenth month on the twelfth day (29:1). January 587 BC.[1]

---

3. a. What are the main features of the prophecy against Egypt in 29:1-12?

_____

_____

_____

b. What is their connection to the occurrences of the "recognition formula" in verses 6 and 9?

_____

_____

_____

You great monster lying among your streams (29:3). A crocodile, the feared creature of the

Nile. In Middle Eastern mythology, the sea monster was "a force of chaos that had to be tamed before the world could be created."[2]

You have been a staff of reed for the people of Israel (29:6). It was Israel's fault for trusting a reed to function as a staff of support; she should have been trusting God. But Egypt was judged for offering support yet being no more trustworthy than a reed staff.

No one will live there for forty years (29:11). Nebuchadnezzar attacked Egypt and carried off exiles to Babylon in 572 BC. About thirty-three years later, King Cyrus of Persia defeated Babylon and gave the exiles permission to go home. If it took the Egyptian exiles seven years to prepare and return home, that would add up to forty years. Egypt never became a great power again.[3]

4. a. Summarize the message of the prophecy concerning Egypt in 29:13-16.

_____

_____

_____

   b. Explain the link to the "recognition formula" in verse 16.

_____

_____

_____

In the twenty-seventh year, in the first month on the first day (29:17). April 571 BC.[4]

As pay . . . as a reward (29:19-20). Nebuchadnezzar thought he was making his own decisions when he attacked Tyre and then Egypt. In a sense he was. But in another sense he was doing what the Lord hired him to do — punish

113

For Thought and Discussion: Look closely at Ezekiel 29:17-21. Why would God want to "pay" or "reward" someone like Nebuchadnezzar for his effort in subduing Tyre? And why should the land of Egypt be the payment?

For Further Study: What additional record do you see of God's judgment against Egypt in these passages: Isaiah 19:1-15; Jeremiah 46:1-26?

Judah's faithless neighbors. In fact, Nebuchadnezzar was doing the Lord's bidding even when he destroyed Jerusalem, so the spoils of Egypt are part of that payment too.

5. What judgment against Egypt is prophesied in 29:17-20?

_____

_____

_____

Make a horn grow (29:21). A horn symbolized strength or a person who had strength (a ruler). Israel would gain "strength and encouragement" when she saw God justly judge Egypt.[5]

For the Israelites (29:21). God's people are His main concern even when He is speaking against other nations.

I will open your mouth (29:21). God will have Ezekiel speak His messages freely, because by then the exiles will at last know Ezekiel has been speaking the truth and will be ready to listen to him.[6]

6. a. What prophecy concerning Israel is given in 29:21?

_____

_____

_____

b. How do you perceive this prophecy's connection to the "recognition formula" in 29:21?

_____

_____

_____

114

Ezekiel 30

7. a. What are the main features of the prophecy against Egypt in 30:1-8?

_____

_____

_____

b. What is their connection to the "recognition formula" in verse 8?

_____

_____

_____

The day of the LORD . . . a day of clouds (30:3). Probably not the day of the Lord when God brings final justice at the end of history. This is probably "a" day of the Lord when God brings justice against Egypt.[7]

8. What further judgment against Egypt is prophesied in 30:9-12?

_____

_____

_____

9. a. Summarize the message of the prophecy concerning Egypt in 30:13-19.

_____

_____

_____

b. Explain the link to the "recognition formula" in verse 19.

_____

_____

115

For Thought and Discussion: When we think about the extended prophecies against Tyre and Egypt in Ezekiel 26–32, what application can we make to our perspective on great military and economic powers throughout later history? Are there lessons in these passages that are relevant for all time?

_____

_____

In the eleventh year, in the first month on the seventh day (30:20). April 587 BC.[8]
_____

10. a. Describe the judgment against Pharaoh and Egypt foretold in the prophecy of 30:20-26.

_____

_____

_____

   b. Explain this prophecy's connection to the "recognition formula" in verses 25 and 26.

_____

_____

_____

Arm (30:21). "The part of the body through which a person acts . . . a symbol of strength." [9]
_____

Ezekiel 31

In the eleventh year, in the third month on the first day (31:1). June 587 BC.[10]
_____

11. Assyria is given as an object lesson for Egypt in 31:1-9. What characteristics of this nation are emphasized in this passage?

_____

_____

_____

Assyria (31:3). Assyria was once a great empire, but Babylon crushed her just two decades before. The same will soon happen to Egypt.

A cedar in Lebanon (31:3). "The tallest of the known trees."[11]

12. Describe the imagery used in 31:10-18 to depict the fall of Pharaoh and Egypt, and explain its significance.

_____

_____

_____

_____

Ezekiel 32

In the twelfth year, in the twelfth month on the first day (32:1). March 585 BC.[12]

13. Describe the judgment prophesied against Pharaoh and Egypt in 32:1-8 and the reason for it.

_____

_____

_____

14. What reaction to this judgment is prophesied in 32:9-10?

_____

_____

_____

15. a. How is the judgment against Egypt further described in 32:11-16?

_____

_____

_____

b. How do you perceive its connection to the "recognition formula" in verse 15?

_____

_____

_____

In the twelfth year, on the fifteenth day of the month (32:17). April 585 BC.[13]

---

16. In 32:17-32, the scene shifts downward to the regions of the dead, where "the hordes of Egypt" are sent (verse 18). According to verses 22-32, who will Pharaoh and Egypt encounter there, and what is the significance of this?

_____

_____

_____

_____

Assyria is there. . . . Elam is there. . . . Meshek and Tubal are there. . . . Edom is there. . . . All the princes of the north and all the Sidonians are there (32:22,24,26,29-30). These fallen nations are the "welcoming party" greeting Egypt as she arrives in the underworld. At this moment when Judah is about to die, it is of some comfort to be reminded that God is Lord even in the realm of the dead.[14]

Meshek and Tubal (32:26). "Territories located in the eastern region of Asia Minor, now eastern and central Turkey. In chapters 38 and 39 they are described as allies of Gog, the chief prince of a confederacy. They are included with the evil nations who will be judged for fighting against God's people."[15]

17. How does Ezekiel 32:17-32 amplify and build upon the earlier words of 31:17-18?

_____

_____

_____

_____

Babylon, too, was God's enemy. So why didn't God give Ezekiel a prophecy against that nation? One reason is that Ezekiel and the other exiles were living in Babylonia and needed the goodwill of their neighbors. Also, at this time God was still using Babylon as His instrument of judgment. Finally, "God wanted to use Daniel, a powerful official in Babylon, to draw the Babylonians to him."[16]

18. What do chapters 29–32 reveal most about the Lord and His character?

_____

_____

_____

19. What would you select as the key verse or passage in Ezekiel 29–32 — one that best captures or reflects the dynamics of what these chapters are all about?

_____

_____

_____

20. List any lingering questions you have about Ezekiel 29–32.

_____

_____

_____

_____

For the group

You may want to focus your discussion for lesson 7 especially on the following issues, themes, and concepts (all of them major overall themes in Ezekiel). How are they further developed in chapters 29–32?

- God's glory and sovereignty
- The depth of human sinfulness
- The certainty, nature, and purpose of God's judgment against sin
- The nature of God's covenant relationship with His people
- The promise of mercy and hope for the future

    The following numbered questions in lesson 7 may stimulate your best and most helpful discussion: 1, 2, 6, 18, 19, and 20.

    And again, remember to look at the "For Thought and Discussion" and "Optional Application" questions in the margins.

1. *ESV Study Bible* (Wheaton, IL: Crossway, 2008), introduction to Ezekiel: "Dates in Ezekiel."
2. Iain M. Duguid, *Ezekiel*, in *The NIV Application Commentary*, ed. Terry Muck (Grand Rapids, MI: Zondervan, 1999), 355.
3. *Life Application Bible*, various editions (Wheaton, IL: Tyndale, 1988 and later), at Ezekiel 29:11-15.
4. *ESV Study Bible*, introduction to Ezekiel: "Dates in Ezekiel."
5. Ralph H. Alexander, *Ezekiel*, vol. 6 of *The Expositor's Bible Commentary*, ed. Frank E. Gaebelein (Grand Rapids, MI: Zondervan, 1986), 893.
6. Alexander, 893; *ESV Study Bible*, at Ezekiel 29:21.
7. Alexander, 895.
8. *ESV Study Bible*, introduction to Ezekiel: "Dates in

Ezekiel."
9. Duguid, 371.
10. *ESV Study Bible*, introduction to Ezekiel: "Dates in Ezekiel."
11. Alexander, 899.
12. *ESV Study Bible*, introduction to Ezekiel: "Dates in Ezekiel."
13. *ESV Study Bible*, introduction to Ezekiel: "Dates in Ezekiel."
14. *ESV Study Bible*, at Ezekiel 32:17-32.
15. *Life Application Bible*, at Ezekiel 32:24-26.
16. *Life Application Bible*, at Ezekiel 32:32.

EZEKIEL 33–34
The Turning Point

1. Read through Ezekiel 33 and 34 in one sitting. What overall impressions do you gain of the text?

_____

_____

_____

_____

Now begin your verse-by-verse study.

Ezekiel 33

Chapter 33 begins the final section of the book, which offers promises of hope after the destruction. The chapter starts by recommissioning Ezekiel as Israel's watchman, God's prophet.[1]

2. According to God's words in 33:1-6, what is a "watchman" responsible for and accountable for?

_____

_____

Optional Application: In what ways has God called you to serve as a watchman over some of His people?

3. From His words in 33:7-9, what does the Lord most want Ezekiel to understand?

Ezekiel 33:7-9 is parallel to 3:17-19, while 33:10-20 parallels 18:19-29. God repeats Himself to underscore the importance of something. These words are among the most important ones for us to take to heart in this book.

---

4. How does 33:1-9 build upon or reinforce the earlier message of Ezekiel 3:17-21?

I have made you a watchman (33:7). In chapter 3, God commissioned Ezekiel as a watchman privately. Here He tells Ezekiel to proclaim publicly that this is his job (see 33:2,7). The exiles are now even more responsible for heeding his warnings, and they have a real chance of restoration if they repent.[2]

5. How does 33:10-20 reinforce or amplify God's words in 18:19-29?

Our offenses and sins weigh us down. . . . How
then can we live? (33:10). The people are on
the edge of despair as Jerusalem is surrounded
by an army and they can no longer be in denial
about the coming judgment.[3]

Turn! Turn from your evil ways! Why will you
die? (33:11). With God, it's never too late to
repent. He's a Person, not a mechanism, and
He deals with us as persons. Despair is never a
necessary option, even though change is sometimes a difficult option for us to persevere in,
and despair sometimes feels easier.[4]

In the twelfth year of our exile, in the tenth
month on the fifth day (33:21). January 585
BC.[5]

**For Thought and
Discussion:** From
what you've seen so
far in Ezekiel of the
mindset of the Jewish
exiles in Babylon, how
do you think they
reacted to the news
in 33:21 of Jerusalem's
fall?

6. How does 33:21-22 confirm God's words to
Ezekiel in 24:25-27?

_____

_____

_____

The city has fallen! (33:21). Now that the worst
has happened, Ezekiel no longer needs to
preach judgment. It's now time to speak about
how the people can live looking forward to the
future. Restoration will be his theme from now
on.

The hand of the LORD was on me, and he opened
my mouth. . . . So my mouth was opened
and I was no longer silent (33:22). Recall
God's words in 3:26 to Ezekiel. Ezekiel's muteness ends just before the news of the city's fall
reaches the exiles. God now gives him six messages that offer hope if the people repent.

Ezekiel 33:21-22 is a potential turning
point for the people, as it is for Ezekiel. But

For Further Study:
Review the people's
words in Ezekiel
33:24. How might
their thinking have
been influenced by
these earlier prophe-
cies: Isaiah 51:2-3;
Micah 7:18-19?

the people still have to choose repentance and life, or stay stuck in their ways that lead to death. In 33:23-29 it becomes clear that the people in Judah are choosing death, and in 33:30-33 it's clear that the exiles are making the same choice.[6]

7. Review God's words to the people left in Judah in 33:23-29.

a. What wrongdoing by the people does the Lord call attention to?

_____

_____

_____

b. What punishment for this does He pronounce?

_____

_____

_____

c. What is the purpose for this punishment?

_____

_____

_____

d. How does this passage overlap with the message given earlier in Ezekiel 18?

_____

_____

_____

The covenant blessings promised to Abraham, including life in the Promised Land, depend on obedience to the covenant commands from Moses. If the

126

people of Judah are continuing to ignore the covenant commands, do they have a right to the land (see 33:26)? God says no.[7]

8. In 33:30-33, what fault does God find with those who have been listening to Ezekiel's prophecies?

_____

_____

_____

_____

My people . . . hear your words, but they do not put them into practice (33:31). This happens today too. People sometimes flock to hear a gifted preacher for the entertainment value but go away with no intention of doing what he says. For the exiles, Ezekiel's sign-acts (like lying on his side) have simply been good theater.

---

9. Does 33:33 imply a coming judgment on God's people? Explain your answer.

_____

_____

_____

_____

10. What does chapter 33 reveal most about the character of God?

_____

_____

_____

_____

For Further Study: With God's judgments in 33:23-29 in mind, what background details do you discover in these passages: Exodus 20:4-5,13-14; Leviticus 17:10-14; 19:26; Deuteronomy 29:25-29? Review also Ezekiel 18:6,10 and 22:11.

For Further Study: How is the situation in Ezekiel 33:30-33 matched by what you see in these passages: Luke 6:46-49; 2 Timothy 4:3-4?

Optional Application: God's desire is that His people "will know that a prophet has been among them" (33:33). Are you spiritually sensitive enough to quickly realize when someone in the body of Christ speaks the truth from God? How can you tell?

For Thought and
Discussion: What
familiar passages
come to mind when
you think of the bibli-
cal image of a shep-
herd with his sheep?

Ezekiel 34

11. a. What does 34:1-6 reveal about God's intentions for the leaders of His people?

_____

_____

_____

b. What specific wrongdoing by Israel's leaders
does God bring to light here?

_____

_____

_____

Shepherds of Israel (34:2). Both political and religious leaders: kings, government ministers,
priests, and prophets.

Take care of the flock (34:2). Leaders are supposed
to care for those they lead "even at the sacrifice
of [their] own desires."[8] This is all too rare,
especially in government.

Strengthened the weak . . . bound up the injured
(34:4). Few political or religious leaders in
the Middle East of Ezekiel's day would have
dreamed of their jobs in these terms. "Rul[ing]
brutally" was typical. But Judah was supposed
to be different. She was supposed to have
learned from the brutal treatment she received
when enslaved in Egypt (see Exodus 1:13-14).
Her leaders were not only forbidden to be brutal
(see Leviticus 25:43,46), they were expected to
help the weak. Had they done that, the other
nations would have taken notice.

My sheep wandered. . . . They were scattered
(34:6). Poor leadership "always leads to the dis-
integration of God's people."[9]

---

12. In 34:7-10, why does the Lord say He is "against" the leaders of His people?

_____

_____

_____

13. What does God promise to do for His people in 34:11-16?

_____

_____

_____

14. What does God promise to do in 34:17-22?

_____

_____

_____

15. What were the correct answers for God's people to give to the questions God asks in 34:18-19?

_____

_____

_____

Optional Application: What can you be praying strategically for those in the body of Christ who have leadership responsibilities? And if you yourself have leadership responsibility, what are the most important lessons for you personally in this passage?

I myself (34:20). God promises both to punish the bad leaders and to make sure that the rank and file start getting what they need.

Fat sheep (34:20). A larger group of people than the shepherds. These are community leaders "who had oppressed the weak with violence and grasped the limited resources for themselves." [10]

16. What does God promise to do in 34:23-24, and what do you see as the significance of this?

_____

For Further Study:
How does Ezekiel 34 compare with God's words about shepherds in Jeremiah 23:1-8?

For Further Study:
How does Ezekiel 34 compare with the words of Jesus in John 10:11-18? How is the "Good Shepherd" concept further taught in these passages: Psalm 23; Isaiah 40:11; Micah 5:4; Hebrews 13:20; 1 Peter 2:25; 5:4; Revelation 7:17?

For Thought and Discussion: With Ezekiel 34:25 in mind, think about the concept of peace. Why do you think this is such a major theme in Scripture?

_____

_____

One shepherd (34:23). The solution to bad leadership isn't an end to political and religious leadership. The solution is good leadership. In place of the bad descendants of David who had ruled Judah, God promised a king like David himself who would rule with justice. Ultimately the Jews came to call this coming shepherd the Messiah. When Jesus proclaimed, "I am the good shepherd" (John 10:14), He was claiming to be the one shepherd promised here in Ezekiel 34, the Messiah.

17. a. What does God promise to do for His people in 34:25-31?

_____

_____

_____

b. In this context, what significance do you see in the "recognition formula" in verses 27 and 30?

_____

_____

_____

Covenant of peace (34:25). A covenant in which the people experience the blessings that flow from being at peace with God, having a whole and restored relationship with Him.[11] Those blessings include safety, a just ruler, enough food, and the other things named in Deuteronomy 28:1-11.

In chapters 35–39, Ezekiel gives four

messages that unfold a picture of what this covenant of peace will look like.[12]

18. What does chapter 34 reveal most about God and His character?

_____

_____

_____

_____

19. What would you select as the key verse or passage in Ezekiel 33–34 — one that best captures or reflects the dynamics of what these chapters are all about?

_____

_____

_____

20. List any lingering questions you have about Ezekiel 33–34.

_____

_____

_____

_____

For the group

You may want to focus your discussion for lesson 8 especially on the following issues, themes, and concepts (all of them major overall themes in Ezekiel). How are they further developed in chapters 33–34?

- God's glory and sovereignty
- The depth of human sinfulness
- The certainty, nature, and purpose of God's judgment against sin
- The nature of God's covenant relationship with His people
- The promise of mercy and hope for the future

The following numbered questions in lesson 8 may stimulate your best and most helpful discussion: 1, 2, 8, 10, 11, 13, 15, 17, 18, 19, and 20.

Look also at the questions in the margins under the headings "For Thought and Discussion" and "Optional Application."

1. Leland Ryken and Philip Graham Ryken, eds., *The Literary Study Bible* (Wheaton, IL: Crossway, 2007), at Ezekiel 33.
2. Iain M. Duguid, *Ezekiel*, in *The NIV Application Commentary*, ed. Terry Muck (Grand Rapids, MI: Zondervan, 1999), 383.
3. Duguid, 383.
4. Duguid, 383–384.
5. *ESV Study Bible* (Wheaton, IL: Crossway, 2008), introduction to Ezekiel: "Dates in Ezekiel."
6. Duguid, 384.
7. Ralph H. Alexander, *Ezekiel*, vol. 6 of *The Expositor's Bible Commentary*, ed. Frank E. Gaebelein (Grand Rapids, MI: Zondervan, 1986), 910.
8. Alexander, 912.
9. Alexander, 912.
10. Duguid, 395.
11. Duguid, 396–397.
12. Alexander, 914.

EZEKIEL 35–36

The Promise of Inward Transformation

1. Read through Ezekiel 35 and 36 in one sitting. What overall impressions do you gain of the text?

_____

_____

_____

_____

Now begin your verse-by-verse study.

Ezekiel 35

This is the first of four messages in which Ezekiel describes what the covenant of peace (see 34:25) will look like. Here he says it will involve removing nations (Edom, for example) that have plundered Judah so that the people can live safely in their own land.[1] This message is paired with the one in 36:1-15 as a contrast between darkness and light.[2]

133

For Thought and Discussion: In Ezekiel 35:14, God says to Edom, "While the whole earth rejoices, I will make you desolate." Is it right for others to rejoice when someone or some nation experiences terrible judgment from God? Why or why not?

For Further Study: What further biblical perspective on Edom can you find in these passages: Numbers 20:14-21; 2 Samuel 8:13-14; Isaiah 63:1-6; Amos 1:11; Obadiah?

Mount Seir (35:2). A mountain in Edom that represents the whole nation.

2. In 35:1-9, what are the major elements in the prophecy against Mount Seir (Edom)?

_____

_____

_____

3. What further elements are added to the prophecy against Mount Seir in 35:10-15?

_____

_____

_____

These two nations (35:10). Israel and Judah. In Edom's eyes they are two separate nations and have been for centuries. In God's eyes they are one nation, and 37:15-23 shows that He intends to make them one again.[3]

We will take possession (35:10). Edom and Israel/Judah have been enemies for centuries because Edom has always wanted to claim the Promised Land as her own.

Anger . . . jealousy . . . hatred (35:11). Edom represents any nation that has hated God's people and has wanted to wipe her off the map.

4. How does the prophecy in chapter 35 amplify and build upon the earlier prophecy against Edom in 25:12-14?

_____

_____

_____

_____

134

5. In this context, what significance do you see in the "recognition formula" as repeated in verses 4, 9, 12, and 15 in chapter 35?

_____

_____

_____

Ezekiel 36

Mountains of Israel (36:1). Recall Ezekiel 6. Chapter 36 is "the comforting counterpart to chapter 6."[4] Also, chapter 35 addressed Mount Seir negatively, and now chapter 36 addresses the mountains of Israel positively.

6. a. In the intricately interwoven message of 36:1-7, how is the fact emphasized that this is indeed a message from the sovereign Lord God?

_____

_____

_____

b. What does the Lord promise to do against the nations surrounding Israel and for what reasons?

_____

_____

_____

I have spoken against the rest of the nations, and against all Edom (36:5). Again, Edom represents any nation that hates God and His people. The downfall of Edom represents the downfall of all who hate God.[5]

For Thought and Discussion: What contrasts between chapters 35 and 36 stand out most to you?

7. a. What does the Lord promise to do for Israel in 36:8-15?

_____

_____

_____

b. What is the significance of the "recognition formula" in verse 11 in connection with these promises?

_____

_____

_____

8. What are the main features of Israel's past as God recounts them in 36:16-20?

_____

_____

_____

To establish a covenant of peace, God can't simply eliminate Israel's enemies, give her a good shepherd-king, and cleanse the land. The people themselves are fatally flawed. They would defile the nation again and disobey a good king. So the covenant of peace requires the transformation of the people themselves: a new heart and a new spirit.[6]

They profaned my holy name (36:20). "This was now not because of anything particular they were doing. . . . Rather, they profaned God's name *simply by being in exile instead of in the land of promise!*"[7]

---

9. In light of Israel's history as stated in 36:16-20, what is the significance of God's statement in 36:21?

_____

_____

_____

I had concern for my holy name (36:21). See also 36:22,32. For Ezekiel, God is showing unde-served goodness toward Israel not because of His love but because of His holiness.[8] There is nothing lovable about the people. God acts because He is wholly other, wholly undefiled, and He wants the nations to know who He is. If He is loving (and He is, as His restorative actions will demonstrate), it is a ferocious, awe-inspiring love that seeks the good not just of His chosen people but of the whole world.

10. a. What does the Lord commit Himself to do in 36:22-23 and for what reason?

_____

_____

_____

b. What is the significance of the "recognition formula" in verse 23 in connection with God's promise here?

_____

_____

_____

11. What is God's promise to His people in 36:24?

_____

_____

_____

137

12. What does the Lord promise to do in 36:25, and what significance do you see in this promise?

_____

_____

_____

13. What does the Lord promise to do for His people in 36:26, and why is this significant?

_____

_____

_____

14. In what ways does God's teaching in 36:26 connect with what He said previously in Ezekiel 11:19 and 18:31?

_____

_____

_____

_____

I will give you a new heart and put a new spirit in you (36:26). The inner inclination to live according to God's ways. The people can't manufacture this in themselves (they've proven that). God will have to change them radically.

A heart of flesh (36:26). "In the Old Testament, 'flesh' is often a symbol for weakness and frailty (Isaiah 31:3); in the New Testament it often stands for the sinful nature as a God-opposing force (as in Romans 8:5-8). Here it stands (in opposition to stone) for a pliable, teachable heart."[9]

15. What promise from the Lord is given in 36:27—and again, what is its significance?

_____

138

_____

_____

For Further Study:
How are God's promises in Ezekiel 36:25-27 reflected in the words of Jesus in John 3:3-21?

I will put my Spirit in you (36:27). God not only cleanses us but puts His Spirit in us so that we are able to live consistently as clean people. The Spirit in us makes us delight in God's commands so that it becomes increasingly natural for us to do what pleases Him. Obedience isn't effortless, but without God's Spirit it would be impossible.

16. In 36:28, what is God's promise to His people, and what is its significance?

_____

_____

_____

17. What does the Lord promise in 36:29-30, and what significance do you see here?

_____

_____

_____

I will call for the grain and make it plentiful. . . . I will increase the fruit of the trees and the crops of the field (36:29-30). "He who lives in God has no unsatisfied desires, but finds in Him all that can sustain, strengthen, and minister to growth, and all that can give gladness and delight." [10]

18. What response by the people is prophesied in 36:31?

_____

_____

_____

You will remember your evil ways and wicked deeds, and you will loathe yourselves (36:31). As we grow in holiness, we see the selfish and ungrateful ways of our past more vividly, and we loathe those ways more. We think about them with shame, but that shame doesn't drive us to despair because we have the joy of forgiveness.

19. a. What reason for these things does the Lord give in 36:32?

_____

_____

_____

   b. What response does He call for from His people?

_____

_____

_____

20. What further promises does God give His people in 36:33-35?

_____

_____

_____

21. What is the significance of the "recognition formula" in the context of 36:36?

_____

_____

_____

I the Lᴏʀᴅ have spoken, and I will do it (36:36).
Recall also 17:24, 22:14, and 24:14.

22. a. What further promise does the Lord give in
    36:37-38?

    _____

    _____

    _____

    b. What is the significance of the "recognition
    formula" in verse 38 in connection with the
    promise here from the Lord?

    _____

    _____

    _____

I will yield to Israel's plea and do this for them
(36:37). Or, "This also I will let the house of
Israel ask me to do for them" (ᴇsᴠ). "The blessings promised . . . will not be given without
our cooperation in prayer." [11] In fact, one of the
chief blessings is that God actually listens to
our prayers. He doesn't close His ears because
they are the demands of selfish people, but
allows Himself to be sought.[12]

23. How would you compare the prophecy in chap-
    ter 36 with the prophecy to the mountains of
    Israel in Ezekiel 6?

    _____

    _____

    _____

24. What does chapter 36 communicate most about
    God and His character?

    _____

    _____

Optional Application: Reflect deeply on the rich truths in Ezekiel 36, especially in regard to their application to your local church and for what God desires there. Based on what you see in this passage, what are the most important prayer requests to offer up for your brothers and sisters in Christ?

25. Chapter 36 has been called the key to the book of Ezekiel. Why might this be so?

_____

_____

_____

26. What would you select as the key verse or passage in Ezekiel 35–36—one that best captures or reflects the dynamics of what these chapters are all about?

_____

_____

_____

27. List any lingering questions you have about Ezekiel 35–36.

_____

_____

_____

_____

For the group

You may want to focus your discussion for lesson 9 especially on the following issues, themes, and concepts (all of them major overall themes in Ezekiel). How are they further developed in chapters 35–36?

• God's glory and sovereignty
• The depth of human sinfulness
• The certainty, nature, and purpose of God's judgment against sin
• The nature of God's covenant relationship with His people
• The promise of mercy and hope for the future

The following numbered questions in lesson 9 may stimulate your best and most helpful discussion: 1, 12, 14, 15, 24, 25, 26, and 27.

Remember to look also at the "For Thought and Discussion" and "Optional Application" questions in the margins.

1. Ralph H. Alexander, *Ezekiel*, vol. 6 of *The Expositor's Bible Commentary*, ed. Frank E. Gaebelein (Grand Rapids, MI: Zondervan, 1986), 914.
2. Iain M. Duguid, *Ezekiel*, in *The NIV Application Commentary*, ed. Terry Muck (Grand Rapids, MI: Zondervan, 1999), 404.
3. Duguid, 405.
4. *NIV Study Bible* (Grand Rapids, MI: Zondervan, 1985), at Ezekiel 36:1-15.
5. Duguid, 406.
6. Duguid, 413.
7. Duguid, 414.
8. Duguid, 415.
9. *NIV Study Bible*, at Ezekiel 36:26.
10. Alexander Maclaren, *Ezekiel, Daniel, and the Minor Prophets*, vol. 7 of *Expositions of Holy Scripture* (Grand Rapids, MI: Eerdmans, 1942), 23.
11. Maclaren, 26.
12. Duguid, 416.

EZEKIEL 37–39
Life and Victory

1. Read through Ezekiel 37–39 in one sitting. What overall impressions do you gain of the text?

_____

_____

_____

_____

Now begin your verse-by-verse study.

Ezekiel 37

2. a. Describe the setting and what Ezekiel sees in 37:1-2.

_____

_____

_____

b. What significance do you see in the exchange of conversation between Ezekiel and the Lord in 37:3?

_____

_____

_____

For Thought and Discussion: Imagine making Ezekiel 37 into a film. How would you depict what this passage tells us?

The hand of the LORD was on me (37:1). This phrase, which often introduces Ezekiel's visions (see 1:3; 3:14,22; 8:1; 40:1), encourages us to compare this vision with those.[1] Note how much more hopeful this one is than those that have gone before.

He led me back and forth among them (37:2). God has Ezekiel examine them closely so that there is no doubt about their deadness.

On the floor of the valley (37:2). The same plain between two rivers (see 3:22) where Ezekiel saw God's glory and received the painful command of muteness. It's a valley of death in the land of exile. It contrasts with the "very high mountain" in the Promised Land that Ezekiel will see in 40:2. Israel must be rescued from the valley of death in order to be "brought into the land of life."[2]

He asked me, "Son of man, can these bones live?" (37:3). Merely asking the question is an invitation to hope. Yet because he has seen the furious judgment God has poured out, Ezekiel can't answer, "Yes, of course. All things are possible for You." That would be too glib. God can make the bones live, but only God knows if God wants to do so.[3] Ezekiel's answer comes from humility.

3. a. What does the Lord command Ezekiel to do in 37:4-6?

_____

_____

_____

b. In connection with this command, what is the significance of the "recognition formula" in verse 6?

_____

146

_____

_____

Prophesy to these bones (37:4). Rather than doing the job on His own, God expresses His power through the word given to His servant, the prophet. Ezekiel will need faith to speak these words.

Breath (37:5). The Hebrew word here (*rûah*) is used ten times in 37:1-14, though it is translated variously as breath, wind, and spirit. The breath of God is His Holy Spirit, who gives life to the dead.

---

4. a. What happens in 37:7-8?

_____

_____

_____

b. What does the Lord command Ezekiel to do in 37:9?

_____

_____

c. What then happens in 37:10?

_____

_____

d. How does the Lord interpret these things in 37:11-14?

_____

_____

_____

e. In connection with these things, what is the significance of the "recognition formula" in verses 13 and 14?

_____

_____

_____

Flesh appeared on them and skin covered them, but there was no breath in them (37:8). When God makes the first man in Genesis 2, He first forms the man from dust and then breathes into him the breath/Spirit of life. Likewise, when God remakes these bones into people, He first forms them and then breaths into them. It's no simple matter to raise the dead, and the Spirit has a "central role."[4] God is "re-creating Israel through the prophetic word and the Spirit."[5]

I the LORD have spoken, and I have done it, declares the LORD (37:14). Recall also 17:24, 22:14, 24:14, and 36:36.

The last half of Ezekiel 37 sums up the messages of hope in chapters 34–37. It also sets up the account of the new temple in chapters 40–48 after evil's final outburst in chapters 38–39.[6] The ten tribes of Israel are even more dead than Judah, because they've been dead for a century, but a God who can raise the dead isn't hindered by time.

---

5. a. What does the Lord ask Ezekiel to do in 37:15-17?

_____

_____

_____

b. What explanations for this action does the Lord give in 37:18-22?

_____

_____

_____

Ephraim (37:16). Israel had for centuries been divided into Judah (with Benjamin) in the south and the other ten tribes in the north. The northern kingdom was usually called Israel, but it was sometimes named for its strongest tribe, Ephraim.

One stick (37:17). In 37:15-28, the word "one" is used ten times. It's the theme of the section.

One nation . . . one king (37:22). The tribes that could never reunite with their old hearts and their merely human kings will reunite with transformed hearts and with the Messiah as King.

One King, One Temple

The unity of God's people must be under one King with one temple. Jesus Christ is our King, and He is also our temple (see Revelation 21:22). In His life, death, and resurrection He accomplished everything the Old Testament temple pointed to (see John 1:29; 2:19-21).

As we grow in submission to our King and treat Him as our temple, Christians grow more unified. Disunity is a sign that we are setting up our own temples under our own control. It's critically important that we see ourselves as one flock under one Shepherd, and live accordingly, centered on Christ and seeking unity with one another. There can be no true unity with those who deny that Jesus is the Son of God or who affirm His lordship with words but deny it with their actions.[7]

149

Optional
Application: Reflect
deeply on the rich
truths in Ezekiel 37,
especially in regard
to their application
to your local church
and what God desires
there. Based on
what you see in this
passage, what are
the most important
prayer requests to
offer up for your
brothers and sisters in
Christ?

6. What further prophecy about the nation is given in 37:23, and what significance do you see in it?

_____

_____

_____

I will cleanse them (37:23). Only God can cleanse them, and He will do it. But they are not passive. He would have cleansed them before the judgment if they had wanted to be cleansed. It's up to them to say yes.

---

7. How does 37:24-25 build upon and amplify the earlier recorded prophecy in 34:23-24?

_____

_____

_____

8. How does 37:26 build upon the earlier prophecies in 16:60 and 34:25?

_____

_____

_____

They will live in the land. . . . I will make a covenant of peace with them (37:25-26). First God's renewed people will live at peace in the Promised Land. Then God will deal decisively with the evil that tries to interfere with that peace (chapters 38-39). Finally, with peace secured, the people will have a new temple (chapters 40-48).

---

9. What is the significance of God's promises in 37:27-28 and their connection to the "recognition formula" in verse 28?

_____

_____

_____

I the LORD *make Israel holy, when my sanctuary is among them* (37:28). The restored temple will be the "crowning blessing" for the people. Its existence will prove that God has made a holy people fit to worship Him.[8]

10. What does chapter 37 reveal most about the Lord and His character?

_____

_____

_____

Ezekiel 38

Ezekiel 38 and 39 — Prophecy Against Gog

Back in Ezekiel 33, God's anger against Jerusalem's sin was satisfied when Jerusalem was destroyed. Ezekiel has been promising new life from the dead. However, what if the story is just like the book of Judges, where a cycle of sin leading to judgment by invading armies keeps repeating? Is this going to be permanent new life followed by permanent security from enemies? Chapters 38–39 deal with that question by raising up a climactic army that God decisively defeats. The cycle is over.[9]

The details of these chapters are obscure, but the overall point is clear. Israel's security rests not on lack of threats but on God's unbreakable faithfulness to defend His people. God is all-powerful; "the human, animal, and natural worlds are all under God's control."[10]

151

11. What does the Lord promise to do to Gog and his army in 38:1-4?

_____

_____

_____

Gog, of the land of Magog (38:2). We don't know who Gog is or where Magog is located. Nor do we know when the events will take place; "in future years" (38:8) is all we are told. Gog appears as a mythic figure of evil allied with seven nations (a number symbolizing completeness) from the farthest parts of the world known to Ezekiel. The attacking nations come from north, south, east, and west: Persia (Iran), Meschek and Tubal (in what is now Turkey), Cush (southern Egypt), Put (northwest Egypt), and Gomer and Beth Togarmah well north of Judah.[11]

---

12. How are Gog's forces described in 38:4-6?

_____

_____

_____

I will turn you around (38:4). God, not Gog, is in charge of these events. The evil ones are happy to play their part, not knowing that God is leading them by "hooks in [their] jaws."[12]

---

13. What actions by Gog's forces are foretold in 38:7-9?

_____

_____

_____

152

14. In 38:10-13, what plans of Gog are foretold?

_____

_____

_____

Living at the center of the land (38:12). This
refers to the spiritual center — "the center of
God's favor" — not necessarily the geographic
center. Jerusalem lost this place through sin,
and now the people have received this place
back.[13]

15. a. What actions by Gog are foretold in 38:14-16?

_____

_____

_____

   b. How is God's sovereignty over Gog demon-
   strated in these verses?

_____

_____

_____

16. a. What actions by God against Gog are prophesied in 38:17-23?

_____

_____

_____

   b. How does this demonstrate God's sovereignty
   over Gog?

_____

_____

_____

153

Optional Application: How do you think Ezekiel 38 relates most to our spiritual warfare today as believers in Christ and soldiers of Christ?

For Thought and Discussion: Imagine making Ezekiel 38–39 into a film. How would you depict what these chapters tell us?

c. In this context, what is the significance of the "recognition formula" in verse 23?

_____

_____

_____

My hot anger . . . my zeal and fiery wrath (38:18-19). Israel has been the target of these earlier in Ezekiel. Now that time is over.

---

17. What does chapter 38 reveal most about God and His character?

_____

_____

_____

_____

Ezekiel 39

18. a. In 39:1-6, what does God promise will happen to Gog and his realm?

_____

_____

_____

b. In this context, what is the significance of the "recognition formula" in verse 6?

_____

_____

_____

19. a. What does the Lord promise in 39:7-8?

_____

_____

_____

b. What is the significance of the "recognition
   formula" (see verse 7) as it occurs in this
   context?

_____

_____

_____

20. What happens in 39:9-10, as foretold by the
    Lord?

_____

_____

_____

Use the weapons for fuel (39:9). Israel has played
no part in winning the fight. She has no army
and no weapons. She takes action only now
that the battle is won, and her action is to plun-
der the corpses. She turns the enemy's weapons to peaceful purposes: cooking and heating
fuel.

21. What happens in 39:11-16, as foretold by the
    Lord?

_____

_____

_____

22. What message for predator beasts and birds
    does God give to Ezekiel in 39:17-20?

_____

_____

_____

Call out to every kind of bird and all the wild animals (39:17). The invading army is not slaughtering the local animals to feed itself. Rather, the invaders are food for the animals.

23. a. What does the Lord promise to do in 39:21-22?

_____

_____

_____

    b. In connection with this promise, what is the significance of the "recognition formula" in verse 22?

_____

_____

_____

24. What greater understanding will result from these things, according to 39:23-24?

_____

_____

_____

25. What are the Lord's promises for His people in 39:25-29, and what is their significance?

_____

_____

_____

26. "The lesson Israel is to draw from these chapters [38–39] is explicitly laid out for them in 39:21-29."[14] What is that lesson?

_____

_____

_____

I will be proved holy through them in the sight of many nations (39:27). Even when He talks about rescuing Israel, God's eye is always on the nations. Israel was chosen not for herself alone but to be a blessing to the nations (see Genesis 12:3), and even when God has to discipline some evil nations, His motive is for all nations to recognize His holiness.

For Further Study: How do you see the themes of Ezekiel 38 and 39 reflected in Psalms 2, 46, 48, and 76?

Optional Application: How do you think Ezekiel 39 relates to our spiritual warfare today as believers in Christ and soldiers of Christ?

27. What do chapters 38 and 39 reveal most about the Lord and His character?

_____

_____

_____

_____

Ezekiel 38–39 depicts the final attack by the forces of evil on the people of God. But in its outlines it is like every attack by Satan on the people of God. We don't need to know who Gog is and when he will appear. Just as we need to resist "antichrists" (1 John 2:18) in all generations, whenever they appear, so we need to look to God to defend us from Satan whenever he attacks. Just as God can turn the armies of Gog into food for crows, so also we can trust Him to take care of us in the midst of any attack Satan throws at us.[15]

28. What would you select as the key verse or passage in Ezekiel 37–39 — one that best captures or reflects the dynamics of what these chapters are all about?

_____

_____

Application: Reflect deeply on what is presented in Ezekiel 38–39, especially in regard to its application to your local church and what God desires there. Based on what you see in this passage, what are the most important prayer requests to offer up for your brothers and sisters in Christ?

29. List any lingering questions you have about Ezekiel 37–39.

For the group

You may want to focus your discussion for lesson 10 especially on the following issues, themes, and concepts (all of them major overall themes in Ezekiel). How are they further developed in chapters 37–39?

- God's glory and sovereignty
- The depth of human sinfulness
- The certainty, nature, and purpose of God's judgment against sin
- The nature of God's covenant relationship with His people
- The promise of mercy and hope for the future

The following numbered questions in lesson 10 may stimulate your best and most helpful discussion: 1, 4, 9, 10, 17, 23, 25, 26, 27, 28, and 29.

Remember to look also at the "For Thought and Discussion" and "Optional Application" questions in the margins.

1. Iain M. Duguid, *Ezekiel*, in *The NIV Application Commentary*, ed. Terry Muck (Grand Rapids, MI: Zondervan, 1999), 426.
2. Duguid, 426.
3. Duguid, 427.
4. Duguid, 427.
5. Duguid, 430.
6. Duguid, 435.
7. Duguid, 440–442.
8. Duguid, 436–437.
9. Leland Ryken and Philip Graham Ryken, eds., *The Literary*

Study Bible (Wheaton, IL: Crossway, 2007), at Ezekiel
  38–39.
10. *ESV Study Bible* (Wheaton, IL: Crossway, 2008), at Ezekiel
    38–39.
11. Duguid, 447–448.
12. Duguid, 448.
13. Duguid, 448–449.
14. Duguid, 451.
15. Duguid, 455–456.

EZEKIEL 40–44
A New Temple

1. Read through Ezekiel 40–44 in one sitting.
   What overall impressions do you gain of the
   text?

   _____

   _____

   _____

   _____

   Now begin your verse-by-verse study.

Ezekiel 40

Ezekiel's Vision of the New Temple (Chapters 40–48)

Ezekiel 40–48 is one of the hardest passages
in the Bible to interpret. It envisions an enor-
mous new temple in Jerusalem, vastly larger
than the one that was destroyed in Ezekiel's
day and vastly larger than the rebuilt temple
of Jesus' day, which was destroyed a few
decades after Jesus' resurrection. Ezekiel's
other visions are full of symbolism (we don't
take the wheeled throne of chapter 1 literally,
for example, and we don't think God is literally
made of glowing metal in the shape of a man).

(continued on page 162)

(continued from page 161)

So it's likely that some or all of the details of this temple are to be taken as symbolizing spiritual realities. But is any of it literal?

Some readers lean heavily toward a literal interpretation. They believe that in a future millennial kingdom on earth, the twelve tribes of Israel will live in the Promised Land, will build the physical structure that Ezekiel describes, and will offer animal sacrifices there as memorials of what Christ did on the cross.

Other readers think Ezekiel's vision symbolizes the blessings God's people will enjoy when God makes the new heavens and new earth (see Isaiah 66:17; 2 Peter 3:13; Revelation 21:1). These readers believe the "the temple represents the orderliness and beauty of God's heavenly dwelling place"; the priests offering sacrifices represent the whole people of God engaged in their most treasured activity, worshipping God; "the river represents the outward flow of God's blessings to his people forever"; and so on.

Still other readers see the temple and the renewed land as an extended metaphor of God dwelling among His covenant people now, the church. They point out passages like Ephesians 2:19-22 that speak of God's people as His temple.

And other readers believe we can't know which elements of the vision are literal or symbolic until we experience the hard-to-describe future realities they represent.

What we can know for sure are the themes of the vision: God's supremacy; His holiness; the requirements of living with a holy God, including personal holiness and communal justice; the people's need to be renewed by the Holy Spirit so that they can be a holy people dwelling with a holy God.[1]

In the twenty-fifth year of our exile, at the beginning of the year, on the tenth of the month, in the fourteenth year after the fall of the city (40:1). April 573 BC.[2] Instead of just giving the calendar date as before, Ezekiel also dates the vision as coming fourteen years after the life-transforming disaster of Jerusalem's destruction and twenty-five years after the start of the Exile.[3]

2. In 40:1-2, what is the setting where Ezekiel is taken?

_____

_____

_____

The hand of the LORD was on me (40:1). Recall the similar wording used in connection with Ezekiel's earlier visions (see 1:3; 3:14,22; 8:1; 37:1).

Visions of God (40:2). See also 1:1 and 8:3.

---

3. In 40:2-3, what does Ezekiel see?

_____

_____

_____

On a very high mountain (40:2). Moses received the design for the tabernacle when he climbed Mount Sinai. Moses also had his only glimpse of the Promised Land when he climbed Mount Nebo just before his death. The destroyed Jerusalem temple had been on Mount Zion.

I saw a man whose appearance was like bronze (40:3). An angel. In chapter 8, Ezekiel had a tour of the corrupted temple and then saw the glory of the Lord abandon the temple. This tour of a new temple will reach its climax when the glory of the Lord comes to it, reversing the judgment (see 43:1-5).[4]

---

4. What is the instruction given to Ezekiel in 40:4?

163

_____

_____

_____

5. Record the most prominent features of the temple area as indicated in each of these sections of chapter 40:

40:5 (wall)

_____

_____

40:6-16 (gateway and outer court)

_____

_____

40:17-19 (outer court)

_____

_____

40:20-23 (north gate)

_____

_____

40:24-27 (south gate)

_____

_____

40:28-37 (inner court)

_____

40:38-43 (rooms for preparing sacrifices)

_____

_____

_____

40:44-47 (rooms for priests)

_____

_____

_____

40:48-49 (temple entrance)

_____

_____

_____

I saw a wall (40:5). More than ten feet high and
ten feet thick, this is the massive wall of a fortress. It separates the holy area of the temple
from the "common" area outside.[5] "Common"
or "profane" in this sense doesn't mean "evil"
or "defiled"; it just means an area in everyday
use that doesn't reach the level of purity of
God's utter holiness. If the idea of holiness is
vague in our minds, this vision of the temple
will give us a feel for how radical God's holiness
is.

A room . . . in each of the inner gateways
(40:38). Solomon's temple was a place of prayer,
not just sacrifice (see 1 Kings 8:28-54; Isaiah
56:7). By giving us details of the rooms for
preparing sacrifices, this vision emphasizes the
absolute importance of offering sacrifices to
atone for sin in order to approach a holy God.[6]

The court . . . was square (40:47). The temple is a
perfect square (perfect symmetry reminds us of

God's perfect holiness). The areas within it are squares within and above squares, so that the most holy place is the highest and innermost square.[7]

Ezekiel 41

6. Describe what features inside the temple are highlighted in each of these sections:

41:1-4 (main interior rooms)

_____

_____

_____

41:5-7 (walls and outer structure)

_____

_____

_____

41:8-11 (side rooms)

_____

_____

_____

41:12 (a separate outer building)

_____

_____

_____

This is the Most Holy Place (41:4). Even before God's glory enters it, this place is too holy for Ezekiel to enter. The angel enters alone, measuring each of three doorways as he goes, each narrower than the last.[8]

7. What measurements for the temple are given in 41:13-15? (See also 40:47.)

_____

_____

_____

8. What aspects of the temple's finish work and layout are given in 41:15-26?

_____

_____

_____

_____

Ezekiel 42

9. Describe the rooms in the perimeter wall around the outer court as detailed in 42:1-14.

_____

_____

_____

10. What are the measurements of the temple area as given in 42:15-20?

_____

_____

_____

He led me out (42:15). Ezekiel now sees the temple from the outside. It is a perfect square (perfect symmetry), 875 feet by 875 feet. Well over four football fields in size.

A wall (42:20). The final comment takes us back to the wall that separates the holy from the common.

For Further Study:
How do these passages show the purpose of the temple finding its fulfillment in Jesus Christ: John 1:5,14; 2:19; 10:17-18; 2 Corinthians 6:16; Ephesians 2:20-21; Philippians 2:7-8; Hebrews 4:15; 7:25?

11. What significance do you see in the final phrase in 42:20?

_____

_____

_____

_____

When the Jews went back to Jerusalem after their exile, they did not follow Ezekiel's description in building the second temple, not even on a smaller and less elaborate scale. It may be built in the future. Consider also how Jesus Himself is the temple, God dwelling with His people in perfect holiness, revealing His glory (see John 1:14), and how the community of Christians is also a dwelling place for God's Holy Spirit (see 1 Corinthians 3:16). Do we take His holiness seriously enough?

Ezekiel 43

12. a. Outline and summarize what happens in 43:1-5.

_____

_____

_____

_____

    b. How do these events serve as a counterpart to what happened in 10:18-22 and 11:23?

_____

_____

The gate facing east (43:1). The glory departed through the east gate (see 10:18-19) and now returns the same way.

The land was radiant (43:2). The glory had filled the previous temple (see 1 Kings 8:10-11), but now it even makes the land shine.[9]

The glory (43:2,4-5). Mentioned four times in four verses, the glory (radiant presence) of the Lord in His holy place makes His people's relationship with Him newly intimate.

13. What is the significance of the words spoken to Ezekiel in 43:6-9?

_____

_____

_____

14. What further significance do you see in the words spoken to Ezekiel in 43:10-12?

_____

_____

_____

Make known to them the design of the temple ... its whole design and all its regulations and laws (43:11). The details of design and regulations matter because they create a living picture of God's holiness.

15. What aspects of the altar are detailed in 43:13-17?

_____

_____

_____

The altar (43:13). The only piece of furniture mentioned inside the temple (see 41:22). It stands "at the geometric center of the temple complex." In the former temple, the altar was outside the Holy Place in the outer court, a lesser place. Here it is given a position of the highest holiness.[10]

16. What regulations regarding the altar are emphasized in 43:18-27?

_____

_____

_____

Purify the altar and make atonement for it (43:20). Merely because it is built of common materials by ordinary sinful humans, the altar will need to be purified of sin before it can be used to worship such a holy God.

No human may enter the Most Holy Place, and the rules of access to the inner court are tighter than the rules for the tabernacle and the former temple. Access depends on the degree of a group's past obedience.[11]

Ezekiel 44

17. What is the significance of the instructions given in 44:1-3 for the gate and the prince?

_____

_____

18. Compare 44:4 with 43:3-5. What is the significance of the repeated elements in these passages?

_____

_____

_____

19. What significance do you see in the Lord's words to Ezekiel in 44:5?

_____

_____

_____

20. What message is Ezekiel given in 44:6-8 to bring to the people's attention?

_____

_____

_____

_____

For Further Study:
How is the concern with "access" to the holy, as noted here in Ezekiel 44, conveyed also in these passages: Psalms 15:1-5; 24:3-6; 27:4; 61:4; 84:4; John 3:3-5; 17:24?

For Further Study:
With Ezekiel 44:9-14 in mind, what record of priestly conflict and failure do you find in these passages: Leviticus 10:1-7; Numbers 16; 1 Kings 1:7-8?

Foreigners uncircumcised in heart and flesh (44:7). Probably foreign guards.[12]

21. What message regarding the priesthood is Ezekiel given in 44:9-14?

_____

_____

_____

The Levites . . . may serve in my sanctuary (44:10-11). Instead of foreign guards, this temple will have guards from the tribe of Levi. The

For Further Study: In Ezekiel 44:15, the Lord refers to the descendants of Zadok as those "who guarded my sanctuary when the Israelites went astray from me." What more do you learn about Zadok and his descendants in 1 Samuel 2:35; 2 Samuel 15:24-29, 35-26; 18:19,22,27; 20:25; 1 Kings 1:39; 2:35; 4:2; 1 Chronicles 6:8-15; 16:39; 24:3; 2 Chronicles 31:10?

Optional Application: What do you learn from Ezekiel 40–44 that relates to your worship of God or to your appreciation of the temple as a picture of Jesus Christ?

Levites are deemed acceptable to simply guard the place, though because of their past sins they will no longer be allowed to do any work with the temple's holy furnishings and utensils.

22. What regulations concerning the priesthood are given in 44:15-27?

_____

_____

_____

_____

Descendants of Zadok . . . who guarded my sanctuary when the Israelites went astray from me (44:15). The Zadokites are not sinless, but they were relatively obedient in the past compared to others from the tribe of Levi. They are good enough to minister at the altar in the inner court. They are still not holy enough to enter the Most Holy Place on the Day of Atonement, as the high priest used to do (see Leviticus 16).[13]

---

23. What provisions for the priests are described in 44:28-31?

_____

_____

_____

24. What is revealed most about God and His character in chapters 40–44?

_____

_____

_____

_____

25. What would you select as the key verse or passage in Ezekiel 40–44 — one that best captures or reflects the dynamics of what these chapters are all about?

_____

_____

_____

26. List any lingering questions you have about Ezekiel 40–44.

_____

_____

_____

_____

For the group

You may want to focus your discussion for lesson 11 especially on the following issues, themes, and concepts (all of them major overall themes in Ezekiel). How are they further developed in chapters 40–44?

- God's glory and sovereignty
- The depth of human sinfulness
- The certainty, nature, and purpose of God's judgment against sin
- The nature of God's covenant relationship with His people
- The promise of mercy and hope for the future

The following numbered questions in lesson 11 may stimulate your best and most helpful discussion: 1, 13, 14, 19, 24, 25, and 26.

Remember to look also at the "For Thought and Discussion" and "Optional Application" questions in the margins.

1. *ESV Study Bible* (Wheaton, IL: Crossway, 2008), at Ezekiel 40–48.
2. *ESV Study Bible*, introduction to Ezekiel: "Dates in Ezekiel."

3. Iain M. Duguid, *Ezekiel*, in *The NIV Application Commentary*, ed. Terry Muck (Grand Rapids, MI: Zondervan, 1999), 470.
4. Duguid, 472.
5. Duguid, 473–474.
6. Duguid, 474–475.
7. *ESV Study Bible*, at Ezekiel 40:1–42:20.
8. Duguid, 476.
9. Duguid, 489.
10. Duguid, 491.
11. Duguid, 500.
12. Duguid, 501.
13. *ESV Study Bible*, at Ezekiel 44:15-31; Duguid, 502.

EZEKIEL 45–48

A New Land

Ezekiel 45

1. Read through Ezekiel 45–48 in one sitting. What overall impressions do you gain of these final chapters?

_____

_____

_____

_____

Now begin your verse-by-verse study.

In chapter 48, the twelve tribes of Israel are going to be resettled in the Promised Land in allotted areas. The priests will have no allotted land because the Lord will be their inheritance. They will live in a holy strip of land that Ezekiel describes in 45:1-8, a strip that runs through the center of the land from the western seacoast to the eastern border. The point of this allotment isn't human rights but divine holiness. This strip will be less holy

175

For Thought and Discussion: What are the most important principles for worship by God's people that are in some way touched on or reflected in Ezekiel 40–48?

than the temple but more holy than the rest of the land.[1]

2. What are the most important features given in 45:1-6 for the sacred district around the temple?

_____

_____

_____

The entire area will be holy (45:1). If the people want to live with the holy God in their midst, this is the kind of regulation they will have to deal with.

---

3. What provisions for the prince are made in 45:7-8?

_____

_____

_____

4. What instructions for Israel's leaders are given in 45:8-9?

_____

_____

_____

5. What is the significance of the instructions given in 45:10-12?

_____

_____

_____

6. In 45:13-20, what are the most important instructions given regarding Israel's offering?

_____

_____

_____

7. What regulations for Israel's holy days are given in 45:21-25?

_____

_____

_____

The first month . . . the seventh month (45:21, 25). Just as Ezekiel's temple lacks most of the furnishings of the former temple, so his calendar in 45:18-25 is stripped down to bare essentials. There is Passover in the first month, but the festival in the seventh month is no longer named Tabernacles, and there is no mention of the Day of Atonement from Leviticus 16.

Ezekiel 46

8. Summarize the regulations set forth in each of these sections of chapter 46:

46:1-8

_____

_____

46:9-15

_____

_____

46:16-18

_____

_____

The prince is to enter . . . and stand by the gatepost. . . . He is to bow down in worship at the threshold of the gateway (46:2). The prince is the one layperson allowed to approach the Lord's house. He is allowed to go as far as the east gate of the inner court. There he prostrates himself on the ground.[2]

The people of the land are to worship . . . at the entrance of that gateway (46:3). The people are much farther away. Between them and where the prince is, there are eight steps up, followed by a ninety-foot corridor. This is as close as they can safely come to God's holy presence.[3] If we take in how awesome God's holiness is, we can better appreciate why the people of Jesus' day found it impossible to believe that He was God living in their midst so approachably.

9. Summarize what Ezekiel experiences and sees in 46:19-24 as well as what he is told.

_____

_____

_____

_____

The place where the priests are to cook the guilt offering . . . to avoid . . . consecrating the people (46:20). Again we have the strong separation between the holy and the common. Meat offered in sacrifice is too holy to cook even in the outer court, where the people are allowed to go. Cleansing all the people enough for them to get near the sacrificed meat would be far too elaborate a process to do regularly. These regulations are for the people's safety. God's holiness can be compared to radioactivity — perfectly good, but dangerous for mere mortals.

178

The sacrifices of the people (46:24). Ezekiel doesn't spell out the sacrifices the people will offer.

It's no small thing to create a place where the holy God can dwell in the midst of ordinary people. As challenging as it is, though, it will have vast benefits, as the rest of the book will make clear. God's presence will transform the land from death to life. The river flowing from the temple (chapter 47) represents this.[4]

Ezekiel 47

10. Summarize what Ezekiel sees in 47:1-6 in regard to the river flowing from the temple.

_____

_____

_____

South of the altar (47:1). A living river flowing out to bless the people with healing thus replaces the great bronze pool in the former temple whose water was used for cleansing (see 1 Kings 7:23,39).[5]

Water that was ankle-deep. . . . A river that no one could cross (47:3,5). It begins as a mere trickle and becomes a "thunderous torrent." Its tiny start is typical of things in the kingdom of God, which is like a mustard seed that grows to a great tree (see Matthew 13:31).[6]

When it empties into the sea, the salty water there becomes fresh (47:8). The Dead Sea is called that because it is too salty even for saltwater fish to survive. Nothing lives in the

For Further Study:
Reflect on the healing power mentioned in Ezekiel 47:12. With this picture in mind, describe the importance given to healing from God in the following passages: Exodus 15:22-26; 2 Kings 2:19-22; Psalm 147:3; Isaiah 57:18-19; Jeremiah 17:14; Hosea 14:4; Luke 4:18; 1 Peter 2:24; Revelation 22:2.

For Further Study:
How would you compare the river of Ezekiel 47:1-12 with the facts and images you see in these passages: Genesis 2:10-14; Psalm 36:8-9; 46:4-5; Isaiah 8:6-8; 48:18; John 4:14; 7:38-39; Revelation 22:1-3?

For Further Study:
Keeping in mind the provision for foreigners in Ezekiel 47:22-23, how do you see God's concern for them expressed also in these passages: Exodus 12:48; Leviticus 19:33; 22:18; Numbers 9:14; 15:15-16; Isaiah 56:6-7; Ephesians 2:12-13,19?

Dead Sea. But this river will bring life from the dead.[7] A river that produces abundant fish and fruit, as well as healing leaves, offers hope of a restored paradise. God's somewhat terrifying holiness is the source of this golden life.

11. In 47:7-12, what else does Ezekiel see in regard to the river?

_____

_____

_____

12. Summarize the most important information given in 47:13-23 about the division of land.

_____

_____

_____

For the foreigners residing among you (47:22). Given how holy the land is in this book and how much emphasis there is on the twelve tribes of Israel, it's notable that even foreign-born people and their children can obtain and inherit land in the Promised Land.

Ezekiel 48

Finally, the land is divided among the twelve tribes. Each tribe gets an equal portion (see 47:14), running in a strip from east to west. The allotments thus run parallel to the holy strip of land and the temple, which occupies the center place. This is very different from the allotment of land in Joshua 14–21.[8]

13. From each of the following sections in chapter 48, summarize the information given regarding the division of land:

48:1-7

_____

_____

_____

48:8-14

_____

_____

_____

48:15-20

_____

_____

_____

48:21-22

_____

_____

_____

48:23-29

_____

_____

_____

The workers . . . will come from all the tribes of Israel (48:19). The city thus represents the tribes' unity.[9]

14. What important information about the city gates is given in 48:30-34?

_____

For Further Study:
What are the most important connections you see between the vision in Ezekiel 40–48 and the one in Revelation 21–22?

Optional Application: What do you learn from Ezekiel 45–48 that relates to your worship of God or to your appreciation of Jesus Christ as our Savior?

15. What important information is given in the book's final verse (48:35)?

The name of the city . . . will be: THE LORD IS THERE (48:35). In one sense, God dwells in His temple, well separated from the city by the priestly zone because of His utter holiness, His otherness and transcendence. But in another sense God's presence radiates outward from the temple, flowing in the healing river and enlivening the city.[10]

---

16. How does the book's final statement reinforce the prophecy given earlier in 37:26-28?

Sinful Jerusalem and her defiled temple have been destroyed and replaced with a city and temple where the holy God can be present. The land corrupted by idolatry and ravaged by Nebuchadnezzar's army has become a land protected from enemies like Gog and abundant with the good things from the river of life.

182

17. What would you select as the key verse or passage in Ezekiel 45–48—one that best captures or reflects the dynamics of what these chapters are all about?

_____

_____

_____

18. List any lingering questions you have about Ezekiel 45–48.

_____

_____

_____

_____

Reviewing Ezekiel

19. Remember again God's reminder in Isaiah 55:10-11—that in the same way He sends rain and snow from the sky to water the earth and nurture life, He also sends His words to accomplish specific purposes. What would you suggest are God's primary purposes for the message of Ezekiel in the lives of His people today?

_____

_____

_____

20. Recall once again the guidelines given for our thought life in Philippians 4:8—"Whatever is true, whatever is noble, whatever is right, whatever is pure, whatever is lovely, whatever is admirable—if anything is excellent or praiseworthy—_think about such things_" (emphasis added). As you reflect on all you've read in the book of Ezekiel, what stands out to you as being particularly true, noble, right, pure, lovely,

Optional Application: Which verses in Ezekiel would be most helpful for you to memorize, so you have them always available in your mind and heart for the Holy Spirit to use?

admirable, excellent, or praiseworthy—and therefore well worth thinking more about?

_____

_____

_____

_____

21. Since all of Scripture testifies ultimately of Christ, where does *Jesus* come most in focus for you in this book?

_____

_____

_____

22. In your understanding, what are the strongest ways in which Ezekiel points us to mankind's need for Jesus and for what He accomplished in His death and resurrection?

_____

_____

_____

23. Recall again Paul's reminder that the Old Testament Scriptures can give us patience and perseverance, as well as comfort and encouragement (see Romans 15:4). In your own life, how do you see the book of Ezekiel living up to Paul's description? In what ways does it help to meet your personal needs for both *perseverance* and *encouragement*?

_____

_____

_____

_____

For the group

You may want to focus your discussion for lesson 12 especially on the following issues, themes, and concepts (all of them major overall themes in Ezekiel). How are they further developed in chapters 45–48?

- God's glory and sovereignty
- The depth of human sinfulness
- The certainty, nature, and purpose of God's judgment against sin
- The nature of God's covenant relationship with His people
- The promise of mercy and hope for the future

The following numbered questions in lesson 12 may stimulate your best and most helpful discussion: 1, 5, 16, 17, and 18.

Allow enough discussion time to look back together and review all of Ezekiel as a whole. You can use the numbered questions 19–23 in this lesson to help you do that.

Once more, look also at the questions in the margins under the headings "For Thought and Discussion" and "Optional Application."

1. Iain M. Duguid, *Ezekiel*, in *The NIV Application Commentary*, ed. Terry Muck (Grand Rapids, MI: Zondervan, 1999), 514-515.
2. Duguid, 519.
3. Duguid, 519.
4. Duguid, 530.
5. Duguid, 530.
6. Duguid, 532.
7. Duguid, 532.
8. Duguid, 544–545.
9. Duguid, 546.
10. Duguid, 547.

STUDY AIDS

For further information on the material in this study, consider the following sources. They are available on the Internet (such as at www.christianbook.com and www.amazon.com), or your local Christian bookstore should be able to order any of them if it does not carry them. Most seminary libraries have them, as well as many university and public libraries. If they are out of print, you might be able to find them online.

Commentaries on Ezekiel

Alexander, Ralph H. *Ezekiel*, vol. 6 of *The Expositor's Bible Commentary* (Zondervan, 1986).

Allen, Leslie C. *Ezekiel 20-48*, vol. 29 in the *Word Biblical Commentary* (Word Books, 1990).

Block, Daniel I. *The Book of Ezekiel*, 2 vols., in the *New International Commentary on the Old Testament* (Eerdmans, 1997–1998).

Calvin, John. *Commentaries on the First Twenty Chapters of the Book of the Prophet Ezekiel*, 2 vols., trans. Thomas Myers, in Calvin's Commentaries (Eerdmans, 1948).

Davidson, A. B. *The Book of the Prophet Ezekiel* (Cambridge University Press, 1900).

Duguid, Iain M. *Ezekiel*, in *The NIV Application Commentary* (Zondervan, 1999).

Fairbairn, Patrick. *An Exposition of Ezekiel* (Sovereign Grace Publishers, 1960).

Greenberg, Moshe. *Ezekiel: A New Translation with Introduction and Commentary*, two vols., in *The Anchor Bible* (Doubleday, 1983–1997).

Hals, Ronald M. *Ezekiel*, vol. 19 in *The Forms of Old Testament Literature* (Eerdmans, 1989).

Keil, Carl Friedrich. *Biblical Commentary on the Prophecies of Ezekiel*, 2 vols., trans. James Martin, in *Biblical Commentary on the Old Testament* by C. F. Keil and F. Delitzsch (Eerdmans, 1950).

Zimmerli, Walther. *Ezekiel: A Commentary on the Book of the Prophet Ezekiel*, 2 vols., trans. Ronald E. Clements (Fortress Press, 1979–1983).

Historical background sources and handbooks

Bible study becomes more meaningful when modern Western readers understand the times and places in which the biblical authors lived. *The IVP Bible Background Commentary: Old Testament*, by John H. Walton, Victor H. Matthews, and Mark Chavalas (InterVarsity, 2000), provides insight into the ancient Near Eastern world, including its peoples, customs, and geography, to help contemporary readers better understand the context in which the Old Testament Scriptures were written.

A **handbook** of biblical customs can also be useful. Some good ones are the time-proven, updated classic *Halley's Bible Handbook with the New International Version*, by Henry H. Halley (Zondervan, 2007), and the inexpensive paperback *Manners and Customs in the Bible*, by Victor H. Matthews (Hendrickson, 1991).

Concordances, dictionaries, and encyclopedias

A **concordance** lists words of the Bible alphabetically along with each verse in which the word appears. It lets you do your own word studies. An *exhaustive* concordance lists every word used in a given translation, while an *abridged* or *complete* concordance omits either some words, some occurrences of the word, or both.

Two of the best exhaustive concordances are *Strong's Exhaustive Concordance* and *The Strongest NIV Exhaustive Concordance*. *Strong's* is available based on the King James Version of the Bible and the New American Standard Bible. *Strong's* has an index by which you can find out which Greek or Hebrew word is used in a given English verse. The NIV concordance does the same thing except it also includes an index for Aramaic words in the original texts from which the NIV was translated. However, neither concordance requires knowledge of the original languages. *Strong's* is available online at www.biblestudytools.com. Both are also available in hard copy.

A **Bible dictionary** or **Bible encyclopedia** alphabetically lists articles about people, places, doctrines, important words, customs, and geography of the Bible.

Holman Illustrated Bible Dictionary, by C. Brand, C. W. Draper, and A. England (B&H, 2003), offers more than seven hundred color photos, illustrations, and charts; sixty full-color maps; and up-to-date archeological findings — along with exhaustive definitions of people, places, things, and events — and deals with every subject in the Bible. It uses a variety of Bible translations and is the only dictionary that includes the HCSB, NIV, KJV, RSV, NRSV, REB, NASB, ESV, and TEV.

The New Unger's Bible Dictionary, Revised and Expanded, by Merrill F. Unger (Moody, 2006), has been a best seller for almost fifty years. Its 6,700-plus entries reflect the most current scholarship, and more than 1.2 million words are supplemented with detailed essays, colorful photography and maps, and dozens of charts and illustrations to enhance your understanding of God's Word. Based on the New American Standard Bible.

The Zondervan Encyclopedia of the Bible, edited by Moisés Silva and Merrill C. Tenney (Zondervan, 2008), is excellent and exhaustive. However, its five 1,000-page volumes are a financial investment, so all but very serious students may prefer to use it at a church, public, college, or seminary library.

Unlike a Bible dictionary in the above sense, *Vine's Complete Expository Dictionary of Old and New Testament Words*, by W. E. Vine, Merrill F. Unger, and William White Jr. (Thomas Nelson, 1996), alphabetically lists major words used in the King James Version and defines each Old Testament Hebrew or New Testament Greek word the KJV translates with that English word. *Vine's* lists verse references where that Hebrew or Greek word appears so that you can do your own cross-references and word studies without knowing the original languages.

The Brown-Driver-Briggs Hebrew and English Lexicon, by Francis Brown, C. Briggs, and S. R. Driver (Hendrickson, 1996), is probably the most respected and comprehensive Bible lexicon for Old Testament studies. *BDB* gives not only dictionary definitions for each word but relates each word to its Old Testament usage and categorizes its nuances of meaning.

Bible atlases and map books

A **Bible atlas** can be a great aid to understanding what is going on in a book of the Bible and how geography affected events. Here are a few good choices:

The Hammond Atlas of Bible Lands (Langenscheidt, 2007) packs a ton of resources into just sixty-four pages. It includes maps, of course, but also photographs, illustrations, and a comprehensive timeline. It offers an introduction to the unique geography of the Holy Land, including terrain, trade routes, vegetation, and climate information.

The New Moody Atlas of the Bible, by Barry J. Beitzel (Moody, 2009), is scholarly, very evangelical, and full of theological text, indexes, and references. Beitzel shows vividly how God prepared the land of Israel perfectly for the acts of salvation He was going to accomplish in it.

Then and Now Bible Maps Insert (Rose, 2008) is a nifty paperback sized just right to fit inside your Bible cover. Only forty-four pages long, it features clear plastic overlays of modern-day cities and countries so you can see what nation or city now occupies the Bible setting you are reading about. Every major city of the Bible is included.

For small-group leaders

Discipleship Journal's Best Small-Group Ideas, Volumes 1 and 2 (NavPress, 2005). Each volume is packed with 101 of the best hands-on tips and group-building principles from *Discipleship Journal's* "Small Group Letter" and "DJ Plus" as well as articles from the magazine. They will help you inject new passion into the life of your small group.

Donahue, Bill. *Leading Life-Changing Small Groups* (Zondervan, 2002). This comprehensive resource is packed with information, practical tips, and insights that will teach you about small-group philosophy and structure, discipleship, conducting meetings, and more.

McBride, Neal F. *How to Build a Small-Groups Ministry* (NavPress, 1994). This is a time-proven, hands-on workbook for pastors and lay leaders that includes everything you need to know to develop a plan that fits your unique church. Through basic principles, case studies, and worksheets, McBride leads you through twelve logical steps for organizing and administering a small-groups ministry.

McBride, Neal F. *How to Lead Small Groups* (NavPress, 1990). This book covers leadership skills for all kinds of small groups: Bible study, fellowship, task, and support groups. It's filled with step-by-step guidance and practical exercises to help you grasp the critical aspects of small-group leadership and dynamics.

Miller, Tara and Jenn Peppers. *Finding the Flow: A Guide for Leading Small Groups and Gatherings* (IVP Connect, 2008). *Finding the Flow* offers a fresh take on leading small groups by seeking to develop the leader's small-group facilitation skills.

Bible study methods

Discipleship Journal's Best Bible Study Methods (NavPress, 2002). This is a collection of thirty-two creative ways to explore Scripture that will help you enjoy studying God's Word more.

Hendricks, Howard and William Hendricks. *Living by the Book: The Art and Science of Reading the Bible* (Moody, 2007). *Living by the Book* offers a practical three-step process that will help you master simple yet effective inductive methods of observation, interpretation, and application that will make all the difference in your time with God's Word. A workbook by the same title is also available to go along with the book.

The Navigator Bible Studies Handbook (NavPress, 1994). This resource teaches the underlying principles for doing good inductive Bible study, including instructions on doing question-and-answer studies, verse-analysis studies, chapter-analysis studies, and topical studies.

Warren, Rick. *Rick Warren's Bible Study Methods: Twelve Ways You Can Unlock God's Word* (HarperCollins, 2006). Rick Warren offers simple, step-by-step instructions, guiding you through twelve different approaches to studying the Bible for yourself with the goal of becoming more like Jesus.

Encounter God's Word
Experience LifeChange

LifeChange by The Navigators

The LifeChange Bible study series can help you grow in Christ-likeness through a life-changing encounter with God's Word. Discover what the Bible says, and develop the skills and desire to dig even deeper into God's Word. Each study includes study aids and discussion questions.